Get Organized, Stay Organized

2018 Edition
Christine D. Shuck

Introduction

"You have to listen to that individual; what do they want from their lives? Not everyone needs to have the classic 1950s perfect little house, but they need help, they need that extra eye and they need someone who will listen to them." —Excerpt from appearance on KCUR radio, The Walt Bodine Show, March 2008

When you look around your house, what do you see? And possibly more important, what do you *want* to see?

Think about that for a moment.

Our vision of how our home should look cannot be dictated by the sleek uncluttered homes we see depicted on magazine covers or in television shows. Instead, we must make our decisions on how we want our home to look and feel, according to our own needs and desires.

That said, we also can, and should, strive for a home in which we can easily find whatever we need. If you are not paying bills on time because you can't find the paperwork or your checkbook, if you have a pantry filled to capacity yet can't find that jar of pickles you bought yesterday, then you probably need a little more organizing in your life!

I'm going to explain to you how easy it is to lose yourself in clutter, what you can do to regain control of your possessions, and how you can live a more organized life.

I will be walking you through this process one step at a time. Whether you have hours to commit to organizing, or just a few minutes out of each day, I can help you get organized and stay that way.

But before we begin, here is a little back story on how I began doing what I do...

An Accidental Beginning

I began a cleaning business, C's Cleaning Services, in October 2005. After nearly two decades in offices, working clerical and customer service jobs, I was ready for a change. And if that meant scrubbing toilets instead of a dull-gray cubicle, then I was in.

As the years passed, I gave birth to my second child, outsourced most of my cleanings to employees and handled the consults and scheduling.

> *"Speak to your strengths. If you believe you can do it and you want it bad enough—jump in. Just jump in and do it."* —My response to a caller's question on how to get started as a professional organizer

The first organizing client I ever had was an 'accidental client.' They called me to schedule a cleaning consult through my housecleaning business and I arrived at the appointed time to find myself faced with an apartment filled to the brim with clutter—there was no room for a cleaning crew to come in and clean, no surface or piece of furniture that was clear and ready to be dusted, no floor that showed except for narrow pathways that led from one room to another.

I walked away from that consult after telling them that I was sorry, but that my staff simply couldn't provide cleaning service to them without some serious de-cluttering first. As I drove home I couldn't stop thinking about that house and how I really wanted to help them. I thought about the organizing business I was planning to open in another year and had that lightbulb moment—why not now? What was I waiting for? It seemed as if I had just received a personal invitation!

Two weeks later, I started 25th Hour Organizing. Sitting together with my mother and a friend, we talked about what we wanted to do and who we wanted to help. We made the bold promise to add an extra hour to our clients' day— "Because 24 Just Isn't Enough." Later that same year, I began teaching the "Let's Get Organized" classes in order to reach out to more of the population in the Kansas City Metropolitan area.

It was the feedback from those classes and the personal requests from my clients and class participants that spurred me to write this book. There is only so much information I could give in a two-hour class, so I began putting together a handout that would fill in for all of the organizing tips we couldn't touch on in class.

That handout grew into the book you now hold in your hands. Whether you have purchased this book while attending my class, off my website or elsewhere, I think you will find it to be a valuable tool in getting you started in your organizing quest.

<u>My First Hoarding Client</u>

It was the summer of 2008 when I stood in a client's house and surveyed one of the worst cases of hoarding I had ever seen. Plastic milk crates filled with books and papers teetered their way to within inches of the ceiling. A hodgepodge of furniture groaning under the weight of papers and books filled the rooms. Pathways, narrow and winding, were the only access to a tiny spot in the living room, a small section of kitchen, and one of the bedrooms. I was told that the entire upstairs was filled with stuff and could not be navigated. I couldn't imagine that it could be worse than the main level, but it most certainly was.

My client and her husband both suffered from OCD and *both* were hoarders. Even as I coaxed them to donate and trash items in the house in an effort to bring their clutter under control, packages would arrive daily, stacking up, unopened, anywhere they could find room.

This client's hoarding tendencies had been building for a while, long before they reached out and asked for help. By the time they did, she was suffering from some rather serious health issues that were exacerbated by the intense level of clutter in her home.

Where do you start when faced with that level of clutter and mess?

The work is more complicated and time-consuming than a simple run-of-the-mill clutter situation, but you have to start somewhere.

You have to really understand something before you are able to teach it. I believe that it often helps if you are able to stand in someone else's shoes and feel what they feel. Perhaps, because I had been organizing and breaking down the process step-by-step nearly my entire life, it came naturally for me to start an organizing business. After all, I had been organizing since I was young, by making a game out of that 'un-fun' task of cleaning my room. Later, I came to love the look of my books, neatly arranged on my bookcase, alternately by author, title or size.

<u>My Own Struggles</u>

"There is a folder of digital pictures on my computer labeled 'weeds.' Weird, but true. We have a big yard and every time a weed pops up I want to pull it and my husband says it's a flower. So we wait. It ends up being a weed; I take a picture of it and keep it in the folder so that next year we don't have the same argument."—Excerpt from a "Let's Get Organized" class at the Christian Legacy Church Women's Retreat—March 2008

I have mentioned in my classes that I am a bibliophile (a book lover) and it is true. When a problem comes up, I figure a book can fix it. One of my lifelong dreams was to have a home library, a special room filled with wall-to-wall books where I can sit and read. I love the feel of books, the texture of their pages beneath my fingers and even the smell of ink and paper. I got that wish in 2013 when we moved out of our small suburban house and into a sprawling Victorian with its own upstairs library.

When shopping, I tend to buy in multiples (shirts in each color offered, for example) and I dread running out of any particular grocery item (such as chicken or hamburger), that I use regularly. I purchase some items almost obsessively: nail clippers, lip balm, pens, even scissors. If the end of civilization came tomorrow, I would probably have enough lip balm to last me five years!

I had long suspected I was born with the 'collecting gene.' I became certain of that fact one day as I stared at my filled-to-capacity bookshelves and embroidery floss collection (did I mention that I have *every* color and shade that DMC manufactures?). Perhaps one of the reasons that I enjoy working with compulsive hoarders so much is because I recognize the symptoms of OCD and compulsive hoarding in myself. I have found myself collecting, letting clutter build up on my desk or kitchen counters in years past. Inevitably I put my foot down and get back on track and clean up the mess. But I understand how painful it can be to let things go at first, and I feel my clients' pain and empathize as I watch them struggle to let their possessions go. I see how difficult it can be for them to stay calm and focused during our organizing sessions.

I believe that with understanding comes empathy, and with empathy can come a resolve to make things better, any way we can. I believe, too, in each individual I work with—each of them has the capacity for infinite growth and change. Often it sits quietly, waiting for the right key to unlock that potential—and that is where I come in.

A few years back I ran across some goal-defining exercises I had written in several different journals. The recurring themes were the same. I wanted to:

- Write creatively (fiction and non-fiction)
- Teach/Share Knowledge
- Help Others

I found that these dreams and goals dated back fifteen years or more. I realized, as I was preparing this book for publication, that I am finally living my dreams. By writing, teaching community education classes and occasionally working with organizing clients—I am actively engaged in 'speaking to my strengths.'

That's an important thing to do—*speak to your strengths*. Build and expand on your good habits, exploit your abilities and push yourself to do something more with your life each and every day. It will make you an effective person and eventually a very happy individual. Belief in ourselves, in our endless potential, is what makes us special. It also makes us stronger.

Client Confidentiality

Despite the prevalence of clutter in so many of our lives, it is often considered to be a sign of inadequacy or shame for many people. I don't believe it is a sign of weakness or laziness or some personal lack in my clients—we all have times when life becomes overwhelming and clutter builds up.

However, I understand my clients' needs for confidentiality and I have done my best to honor that need throughout this book. It is out of respect for each of the people I have worked with that all client names have been changed to protect their privacy. However, their individual stories, and unique situations remain intact.

Are You Ready?

So are you? Are you really ready for a change? You see, it isn't enough to say, "I need to change." You have to really *want* change before it will happen. You also need to have the tools for change. This book provides that and more.

I have divided this book into four sections:

Section 1—Before We Begin Organizing

Section 2—Get Organized

Section 3—Stay Organized

Section 4—Resources

I will show you how to prepare for organizing every area of your home. I will also take you room-by-room and give you tips on how each space is organized on an individual basis. Once you are organized, I will provide ideas for lifestyle changes, simple little alterations in your routine that will ensure you stay organized for months and years to come. The last section will guide you towards important resources that will help you along your organizing journey.

Please remember that becoming organized and staying that way, takes time and effort. But you *can* do it. If you are ready to change your life, and watch a good deal of the stress and frustration from the clutter in your life melt away, then read on.

Happy Organizing!

Section 1: Before We Begin Organizing

How Did It Get This Bad?

"If you have a pile of papers in your room your energy automatically dips because you know it needs attention...every time you walk into your home and there are things that need repairing, letters that need answering, junk that needs clearing, your energy can't flow internally because of what is happening externally." —Karen Kingston, Space Clearer

So really, how *did* it get this bad?

Most of us find ourselves asking that very question at some point in our lives. Even the most organized, energetic and proactive person is going to have moments when life, with its accompanying lumps and bumps, stops them dead in their tracks. That 'dead stop' that we find ourselves in might take days, months, even years to overcome. Meanwhile, the clutter grows and grows, invading our lives, silent and insidious.

But you will find that it is more than just 'life' that contributes to clutter. Face it, we live in the good old United States of America, land of the 'freedom fries' and home of the almighty consumer.

We the Consumer

To properly understand the level that consumerism has invaded even the most frugal American lifestyle, I urge you to look up "The Story of Stuff" on the internet. Just type 'the story of stuff' into a search engine and you will find a link. The presentation is around twenty minutes long and it addresses how we were quietly (and not so quietly) steered towards the level of out-of-control spending and debt that we currently find ourselves in.

'We the people' has become 'we the consumer' and it is eating us alive through good money thrown away on the fad of the day and an overabundance of 'must haves' that we don't really need.

My clients don't like to hear that they don't need twenty pairs of black pants, fifteen silk dress shirts or fifty pairs of shoes. But when your closets are full to bursting, when you don't even recognize a piece of clothing as yours (or can't remember ever wearing it) and you see dust on your clothes and hangers because they haven't been worn for so long, I'm the one who gets to break it to you—*you have too much stuff.*

Everywhere we look, the message is:

Buy me I'll make you look fantastic, sexy and irresistible.

Buy me I'll make you feel young again.

Buy me or don't you want your children to have what you didn't have?

Buy me I'll take payments with a special introductory 0% interest for 90 days.

Buy me,

Buy me,

Buy me,

BUY ME!!!!

I find it especially ironic that we now have a huge industry that provides organizing solutions. See, first they convince you to buy and buy. Then when you run out of room, they sell you something to store it in! And in case all of those storage solutions don't work out—why you can just get a storage space down the street and fill that up too!

There is even an industry devoted to 'organizing.' There are books on how to get organized. You happen to be holding one right now. Then of course, there are professional organizers like me: I earn a living, helping people to get organized.

So here you are. Maybe your closet is a mess or maybe you haven't seen parts of your floor in years. Take a long look around your house and answer me this...

Who Owns Who?

Your possessions should not own you. And when you get to that point [when] you look around and you realize 'I'm adjusting my life around my possessions...I'm not inviting friends over, I'm not able to get into a room in my house...[then] it's time for a change."—Excerpt from appearance on KCUR radio—The Walt Bodine Show, March 2008

Having *things* is a sign of wealth in America. We have gotten so used to the idea of showing off our *things,* that we now buy *things* just to stack in corners. Decorative boxes with nothing in them, wall hangings, knickknacks, glassware in every color of the rainbow and on and on.

Every surface becomes littered with knickknacks, every closet has become stuffed and now we regularly rent storage space for the extra stuff we don't have time to go through and yet, can't bear to part with.

- If you can't see your furniture or open your closet doors...
- If you can't remember *what* is in your closet or what your furniture looks like...
- If you have no idea what happened to your favorite [fill in the blank]...
- If you are embarrassed to have people over...
- If the idea of parting with your possessions induces mind-numbing panic...

Then your belongings may, in fact, own you.

I teach "Let's Get Organized" classes to a wide variety of participants in the Greater Kansas City Metropolitan area. Everyone has different needs or objectives for being at the class, so before I dive into any tips and suggestions on organizing homes I ask my class participants to tell me a little about themselves. "What's bothering you most about your home? What is the biggest issue or reason you are here today?"

Live Your Truth

I am so proud of those participants who introduce themselves at the beginning of class and say, "I'm a compulsive hoarder" or "my possessions own me." I'm proud of them in part, because I understand how difficult it is for them to admit that reality to themselves and especially to others. Recognition or acceptance that there is a problem is half of the battle. I also believe it indicates that at some level, these individuals truly want their lives to change.

I've already said that you have to really want change in your life, for it to really stick. And even if you want it, you still have to work hard at it, sometimes very hard, for those changes to happen. I've seen clients who were pushed into hiring me by family members or friends. Usually there is little I can do for someone who doesn't want to change. If they don't see it as a problem, there will be little if any change in behavior. The person who knows and accepts there is a problem, is far more likely to be open to eradicating the clutter because they want their life to be different. And that is a beautiful thing to be a part of.

In case you have not heard of compulsive hoarding, or would like a better explanation of the condition, let me give you an overview:

OCD and Compulsive Hoarding

Obsessive-compulsive disorder (OCD) is a type of anxiety disorder. Anxiety disorder is the experience of prolonged, excessive worry about circumstances in one's life. OCD is characterized by distressing repetitive thoughts, impulses, or images that are intense, frightening, absurd, or unusual. These thoughts are followed by ritualized actions that are usually bizarre and irrational. These ritual actions, known as compulsions, help reduce anxiety caused by the individual's obsessive thoughts. Often described as the "disease of doubt," the sufferer usually knows the obsessive thoughts and compulsions are irrational but, on another level, fears they may be true.—http://www.reference.com

It is estimated that approximately 1% of the world's population suffers from obsessive-compulsive disorder (OCD). Of that number approximately ¼ to 1/3 also have compulsive hoarding tendencies. Oddly enough, here in the United States, approximately 2.5% of the population suffers from OCD. Is there any link between our consumer mentality and compulsive hoarding? Perhaps, perhaps not. At present, there are no studies addressing that particular question.

So let me break down those figures into more manageable bites. I currently reside in an average-sized city in the Midwest - Kansas City, Missouri.

In 2017, the population of the Greater Kansas City Metropolitan area was approximately 2,340,000. If Kansas City follows the nation's average, then at least 58,500 individuals in this area suffer from obsessive-compulsive disorder. OCD can manifest itself in a variety of ways—something as simple as repetitive hand-washing or an unusual inflexibility in deviating from certain daily rituals (see definition in box above). This also means that up to 17,500 people in the Greater Kansas

City Metropolitan area alone, maybe more, could be compulsive hoarders.

Compulsive hoarding (or pathological hoarding) is extreme hoarding behavior in humans. It involves the collection and/ or failure to discard large numbers of objects even when their storage causes significant clutter and impairment to basic living activities such as moving around the house, cooking, cleaning, showering or sleeping. —Wikipedia

We aren't counting the near infinite number of cluttered kitchens or packed closets here—we are talking simply of the 17,500 individuals in one metropolitan area who suffer from a *severe* form of clutter!

According to several studies, those numbers could be even larger. Due to the shame and embarrassment that accompanies this situation, we find that many individuals never seek help and the clutter continues to build—often with fatal consequences.

It was so cluttered in a home that caught fire last night in Carlsbad, Calif., that firefighters couldn't even get inside at first—and once they did, it was too late to save the elderly woman who lived there. – Newser, November 2014

And there was this news report from October 2007:

It took a 14-person chain of firefighters to pull 90-year-old Michael Halko out from under heaps of boxes, newspapers and trash in his Norton, Mass., home last week. According to neighbors, he was buried so deep rescuers could see only the top of his head. —Excerpt from 2006 news article

Thanks to recent profiles on compulsive hoarding by well-known personalities such as Oprah Winfrey, Hoarders, and other organizing shows found on HGTV, The Learning Channel and Oxygen—many people now have a basic idea about what compulsive hoarding is. But what do we know about the individuals?

I think it is important to know how people tick. Understanding how a person thinks, means that I can often approach them in an effective, non-threatening manner and get better results. For most compulsive hoarders, their reasoning for keeping clutter falls into one (or more) of these four categories:

- Fear of loss of information (paperwork, emails, articles, magazines)
- Sentimental (a matchbook from their favorite restaurant)
- Just in Case—"I might need it someday!"
- Aesthetic—Bottle caps, twists of paper, anything that catches their fancy

Fear of loss of information

This is a huge problem for nearly every client I have dealt with, and it is spreading as fast as our internet connections. As much as I love the wealth of information I can find on the internet, I have to wonder if too much information can be a bad thing! This is not limited to compulsive hoarders and I will address it (fear of loss of information) and how to deal with the stacks and stacks of paperwork, in a later section of this book.

Sentimental collecting

This can be everything from boxes of belongings from a departed loved one who has passed away, to an object with no intrinsic value that simply reminds us of a certain event or day. For example, I've had a plastic Tigger toy on my dresser for years.

I was working for Children's Mercy Hospital and had to take my daughter to work one day to participate in a research study. While she was waiting, she made a crown and robe for the toy out of paper and taped it carefully onto Tigger. Twelve years later, I still keep it. Take that little Tigger and multiply it one-thousand-fold and you will begin to see the problem in sentimental collecting!

Just In Case

If I had a dollar for every item someone was keeping 'just in case' I would be a millionaire! I see clients who keep clothing and shoes that they haven't been able to fit into in years. I also see motors and parts to broken appliances that the clients no longer own, and innumerable storage containers of various shapes and sizes.

Yes, sometimes these items do come in handy, but at what cost to your health, stress levels and living space? The clients I meet can usually point out one or two examples to justify keeping rooms full of 'just in case' items. And while they are right, they were able to find a use for one or two of the 'just in case' items, a majority of them will never be used and are just wasting valuable real estate.

Aesthetic Collecting

I like to refer to particular form of collecting as the 'curse of the magpie.' Anything shiny, colorful, unusual or of a particular texture may be kept. Like birds, compulsive hoarders will pick these items up, even actively look for them, and then drag them back to use to feather their nests. Of all the items that compulsive hoarders collect, these have the least intrinsic value and are also the hardest to part with.

In my work as a professional organizer I have found that most compulsive hoarders also show core fundamental traits. All of the compulsive hoarders I have worked with were:

- Intelligent
- Strong-Minded
- Perfectionists

You may be questioning the idea of someone existing in almost unlivable clutter as being a perfectionist, but look at it this way. Usually, these individuals have trouble finding the perfect *place* for their possessions. So they place them in a 'temporary' location until such time as the perfect place reveals itself. That perfect place never appears and soon there is so much clutter that closets (and entire rooms) are blocked and the items disappear beneath a mound of other belongings that don't have a 'perfect' home either.

So how did they get to where they are now?

Compulsive hoarders often have a 'trigger' such as:

- Illness (physical and/or mental)
- Death or loss of friend/family member
- Divorce
- Trauma (such as car accident, assault, or even fighting in a war)

"You aren't the first professional organizer I've hired. I had one come here last year and she looked around and said, 'What we need to do is back up a truck to the house and just start tossing this stuff.' I never had her come back. This stuff isn't trash!" – A compulsive hoarding client during an initial consult

The worst thing you can suggest to a hoarder is that their possessions are junk or that the clutter just needs to be hauled away. It offends them, at the very least, and puts them on the defensive. The mental image of losing all of their treasures can be absolutely terrifying. So if you have a friend or family member who fits the compulsive hoarding profile, consider changing your wording and your approach.

Just like non-hoarders, compulsive hoarders deserve the opportunity to have an oasis of calm in their home. They need help in learning to make lifestyle changes that will help them avoid clutter in the first place and they need understanding and compassion for dealing with the clutter they now have.

The most important thing to realize is that compulsive hoarding is rarely a lifestyle *choice*. Hoarders don't want clutter. They have it and they don't know what to do with it and they find it overwhelming. Patience and empathy will go miles farther than ultimatums or frustration when dealing with this problem.

Now for most of you reading this book, you probably do not suffer from OCD or compulsive hoarding. Instead you will be quick to point out that you just have a 'little bit' of clutter. So how does your 'little bit' of clutter affect you and how did it 'get this bad'?

Avoidance/Lack of Decision-Making

Me: Keep or garage sale?

Client: Oh, isn't this piano lovely? I bought it and thought that I would take lessons or send my grandkids to lessons, but we just haven't gotten around to it. It was such a good deal and...

Me: How long ago was this?

Client: Five years ago. I bought it at this garage sale down near the Plaza and this man was so nice, he...

Me: So...garage sale?

Client: Oh...I just don't know. I mean, I might still take lessons.

Me: Okay, when *are you going to schedule the lessons?*

Client: Oh, well, I just don't have time right now—I'm so busy with other things.

Me: So...garage sale?

Client: I guess...do you think I should sell it?

—Conversation during an organizing session with a client.

Many of the clients I see don't suffer from compulsive hoarding, but they definitely exhibit a great deal of stress when faced with decisions. Since organizing is around 90% decision-making and only 10% movement (moving the items from one area to another), you can understand just how hard it can be for those individuals, who have difficulty making decisions.

Take the conversation in the box above. This was for ONE item. The client had hundreds of items that she needed to make decisions on, in order to prepare for an upcoming garage sale. At one point the client asked, partly in jest and partly out of desperation, "Couldn't you just make the decision for me?" I smiled at that one, but my response was, "No. You have to make the decision. These are your personal belongings. I can make recommendations, but I can't make the decisions for you."

Before long I would ask, "Keep or garage sale?" Her job was to simply answer the question. After two hours of this, she was literally shaking in her shoes from the stress.

I have a great deal of empathy for my clients and don't like to see them distressed. Sometimes I feel like the doctor who has to administer a shot to a terrified child. I know it is for their own good, that the clutter is limiting their lives and preventing the oasis of calm that a home should give them. I understand quite well that this is a difficult process, but in the end, that it needs to be done.

Clutter – Cause and Effect

"I call it C.H.A.O.S.—Can't Have Anyone Over Syndrome."—a class participant's notes on our feedback form

Our lives become cluttered for a variety of reasons. We have busy lives, even stay-at-home moms have to keep day planners to keep track of their children's activities. Most of us work outside the home, zipping off to work in the wee hours of the morning and returning late in the afternoon. Cleaning and organizing are usually not as high on our list of priorities as are spending time with the kids, relaxing or getting a meal on the table. And that's just normal life. Here is just a small sample of reasons my clients and class participants tell me about their lives and how their clutter began to take hold:

"There is never enough TIME."

"Everything was fine until I got sick and then things just got out of control."

"My mother-in-law passed away and we had to clear out her house, somehow it all ended up in my house."

"I lost my parents and my sister in the same year and I just so depressed. I couldn't bear to part with any of their things."

"My mother lived through the Great Depression and she taught me never to waste. There's a use for everything and we shouldn't just throw things away when they're broken."

"I don't know how it got this bad. It feels like I woke up one day and it was here, there, EVERYWHERE!"

Clutter builds up when we are ill, when we suffer loss or trauma and when we are busy with day-to-day life. And who doesn't experience at least one of these conditions? Recently, I spoke to a pediatrician who commented, "My patients' parents—from office workers to CEOs—all say the same thing—'I never have enough *time*.'" And time is the biggest issue of all. How do we find the time to clean up the clutter or to avoid clutter in the first place—and how do we organize our lives so the clutter doesn't return?

I won't lie to you and say it is easy. I won't promise you a magical solution. Being organized takes time, patience and a commitment to change. Often it also involves lifestyle changes. Keep in mind, your clutter didn't appear overnight, and it won't disappear in the blink of an eye, it will take effort. The important part is not *finding* the time but *creating* the time to get and stay organized. We will talk about this concept in more detail later. For now, let's return to the subject of clutter and how it affects us.

So our houses are cluttered—be it the garage or the closet or just everything. How does this affect us? I asked some of my clients to describe their feelings in regards to their homes or possessions. And before you read what they said, take a moment to think about your own situation—how does it make *you* feel? When you look around your house and see clutter or piles of stuff, what do you think about or say to yourself?

My clients and the participants in my classes tell me:

> *"I get up in the morning thinking, 'Today will be different, I'll clean up this mess' and then I see the mess and I just feel exhausted. I'm ready to go back to bed!"*

> *"I just don't know where to begin!"*

"I know I need to do something, but I put it off and then I'm angry at myself and disappointed. I never seem to get the energy up to do something about it."

"It makes me crazy. I can't live like this, but I don't know what to do with it all."

Clutter affects us mentally and physically. It is emotionally exhausting to see piles of stuff that has no real home and this causes anxiety and depression, which takes its toll physically. I call it the 'tiger chasing its tail':

Clutter = Anxiety/Stress/Depression = Exhaustion = More Clutter

It's high time to stop the cycle. Your life can be so much better, far less stressful, if you can just learn how to reduce the clutter.

Are You Avoiding Waste or Just Over-Saving?

Part of reducing clutter is determining what items you are keeping and why. I understand the need to be thrifty and when possible, to re-use items for a new purpose.

However, many of my clients have slowly built up a mass of things that have no real value, but that they have difficulty discarding. Their reasons vary:

> The client with three toasters on his kitchen counter: *"Well, this toaster just needs to be repaired, this other one I use for bread, and this one here is for bagels."*

> From the client with a broken kitchen chair: *"I just need to glue the leg back onto the chair."* (The chair broke five years ago)

> When asked why there were over twenty empty water bottles on her counters and filling one sink: *"Well, you can re-use those water bottles."*

I can relate to all of these concerns. I too have difficulty discarding something if it is still useful. Even after it has outlived its usefulness with me, I think that someone else should be able to use it. For example, the idea of throwing away intact, usable clothing, which I have seen some people do, is simply unimaginable to me.

> Wife: *"I keep the empty beer bottles so that we can use them for home brewing."*—the husband told me later they had enough bottles to last them through six months straight of home brewing...and that they hadn't brewed in years.

Or the regularly recurring theme of cluttered homes everywhere: *"I can't throw away these papers until I have read them and understand them completely. What if I lose something important?"*

That said—how do we differentiate between keeping some items to recycle or re-purpose and keeping so many items that our homes and lives are overrun with clutter?

Living in our 'we the consumer' society has some nasty side effects. More and more, people are sensing how much waste we are creating and wanting to stop it by re-purposing items and giving them second and even third lives. The problem arises with time and opportunity. If you don't have time *today* to re-purpose those glass bottles into homemade bottled beer, what makes you think *tomorrow* will be that much different?

As individuals, we need to learn a balance between what we *want* to do, what we *dream* of doing and what we can *realistically accomplish*. So if you are keeping multiples of anything, if it has been sitting and sitting (gathering dust and taking up space), ask yourself: "When am I going to use this?" If you can't realistically envision a time in the next week, month, or year—strongly consider selling, recycling, or donating it.

Does it Matter to You Where it Goes?

"Did you know that they sometimes send those clothes overseas to be made into rags? I never donate to them because of that!" — "Let's Get Organized" class participant responding to my advice to donate clothing to a local charity.

For many of the clients I meet, it matters deeply to them where items go once they leave their homes. Specific charities are often preferred; certain paper must be shredded while other paper may go in the trash. Furniture and other belongings of worth (worth as defined by the owner) are often agonized over as they try to decide whether to sell it or which person or charity deserves it more.

My concern with this obviously difficult decision-making process is two-fold:

1. Clients over-think this issue as a coping mechanism—they don't want to let go of their stuff!
2. Indecisiveness breeds clutter—as long as you delay, the clutter stays and continues to interfere with your life

The reasons I hear from my clients can usually be categorized into three main concerns:

Money—I paid good money for this. If I throw it away or donate it, I've thrown away good money.

Trust—How can I trust someone to take care of my [clothing, etc.] as I would? How can I see that it gets to the right person?

Need—I might need it someday!

These are all valid concerns. I understand them and I too have experienced each of them. I will address these concerns in order.

Money:

I paid good money for this. If I throw it away or donate it, I've thrown away good money.

Yes, you paid good money for this. You have paid good money for most of the items in your home but you keep them now at what cost? How much does it cost you in stress, in anxiety and even physical health (allergies, asthma, etc.)? Or what about the physical exhaustion that you feel when you are faced with that seemingly unapproachable stack of belongings that *aren't being used*? How much does it cost you in space you *no longer have*?

Keep in mind that there is also a big difference between 'cost' and 'value.' What an 8-track tape or 5.5 inch floppy cost you years back was significant—nowadays you can't even *give* those items away.

I know we are a nation of consumers, but the reality is that yes, you can have *too much*. You *don't* need twenty pairs of black pants, or blouses in every color of the rainbow in varying sleeve lengths. You *don't* need a television in every room or a special hot dog cooker (unless you subsist solely on hot dogs, in which case, go right ahead) or an espresso/latte machine right next to your Gevalia coffeemaker on your kitchen counters.

If you really can't let it go without at least trying to recoup some of your investment (keep in mind this will be pennies on the dollar) then please commit to the following:

- Look up consignment shops and consider selling your items at www.ebay.com or www.craigslist.com or having a garage sale.
- Set a 'sell-by' date and stick to it. If it doesn't sell by a week before that date then cut the price drastically. If it still doesn't sell, donate it! (Or put a 'free' sign on it at your next garage sale)

Trust:

How can I trust someone to take care of my [clothing, etc.] as I would? How can I see that it gets to the right person?

The short answer is that you can't always know that your belongings are going to a good place or a good person. But that's not the question you should be asking yourself. Perhaps what you should be asking is:

- Why is this item so important to me?
- Do I remember some special memory when I see this object?
- Does letting go of this item feel as if I am letting go of a memory?

Even if you can't think of a particular reason why you are reluctant to let go of something, keep in mind that objects are not friends or companions, they are just *things*. They can't love us back or keep us company; they are there to benefit our lives. If the benefit of an object ceases, then it needs to go away.

Need:

I might need it someday!

Yes, you might need it someday. You might need that 30th pair of loafers or your 'fat' clothes you haven't worn in five years or the 'skinny' clothes you haven't worn in ten. You might need an empty margarine tub to use for leftovers, so why don't you go ahead and pick it out of the stack that is tipping over there in the corner. Yes, your tried and true coffeemaker *may* die and you'll need that extra one that is sitting in the garage.

But I'm going to tell you what you need more than anything else… space. You need space to breathe. You deserve space to live and a life with room to put plates at the table and open counter space to prepare food. And yes, you need a closet that you can not only step into but *find* things in.

Is the item being used right now? If not, then ask yourself how important it is to keep. The important things in our lives should not be in boxes or stacked in corners—they should be at our fingertips, reminding us of why we found them special, unique or just plain handy. And that leads us straight to the emotional keepsakes, the family heirlooms—things that we keep because of the memories associated with those who have gone before us...

Family Heirlooms

"I had just purchased this rocker and my mother came for a visit and commented on how wonderful it was and how comfortable. The next time I saw her I brought it to her to keep. Every time I visited her house, I would make a beeline for the rocker and sit in it while we visited. After she died, I just kept it, I couldn't bear to give it away even though I didn't have any room in my house for it anymore." —A client's answer as to why she was keeping a rocker in her garage

When my maternal grandmother passed away in 2001, I helped my mother clear out her house. I ended up with box after box of her sewing and crafts fabric, a steamer trunk packed full of more fabric and her sewing cabinet. Every once in a while, I would go down to the basement, open a box and just smell my grandmother in the fabric. It was reassuring somehow, and although I didn't have a use for most of the fabric, I couldn't bear to get rid of it.

I did end up making several quilts out of the fabric in those boxes. I incorporated her thread and needles and her sewing machine cabinet into my home, sifted through patterns that included outfits my mother wore in high school and was delighted when I found a pack of World War II era sewing needles in their original case. I was reminded of her each time I sat down at the sewing cabinet to sew or craft a new project.

Eventually, after several years of procrastination, I donated a large amount of the cloth to a local charity. I knew I couldn't possibly use all of the fabric, and I often think about who might have bought it and what they may have created. I know I made the right decision to pass it on, even if it wasn't easy to do at the time.

Family heirlooms, whether it is furniture or knickknacks or personal items—should be proudly displayed or used. When we place them in a box or stuff them in a corner of the basement, how, exactly, are we honoring the memories of our loved ones? What message are we giving ourselves and others about the worth of our (and their) memories?

If you inherit a quilt, *use* it. Use it until it is falling apart and then make it (or have it made) into a stuffed bear and display it for all to see. If those family heirlooms aren't being used or displayed—if you are storing them away where insects and time can eat away at them, then they aren't worth much to anyone... *not even you*. We cannot show respect for our loved ones by keeping these memories boxed away.

Here are some ideas for keeping the memory alive without filling up your home with another person's lifetime of mementos...

Shadowboxes

Shadowboxes are a lovely way to encapsulate just a few knickknacks together that visually tell a story about a loved one. My grandmother loved anything that was purple and won several blue ribbons for her beautiful violets. She canned her own fruits and vegetables, crocheted afghans, enjoyed playing bridge and sewed a good deal of her own clothing. I used a scrap of purple paper to line the back of a shadowbox and inserted a miniature coffeepot with violets printed on it, to signify the coffee set she would serve at a bridge game. I included a miniature can of food to represent her canning abilities and a miniature version of her signature afghans which I crocheted myself out of some purple variegated embroidery floss from the crafts collection I inherited from her. To finish it all off, I included one of her thimbles, a miniature blue ribbon and a black and white photo of her standing proudly before her winning plants sometime in the late '50s.

I found that the shadowbox summed up a great deal of what I knew about her. It was a snapshot of her interests, her joys and her accomplishments. It also helped me to let go of the bolts of fabric I would never use and allowed me to display her memory on a wall where I could see it daily—something that wasn't happening by storing all of those items in the basement.

You don't have to know how to crochet to create a shadowbox. You don't even have to be particularly 'crafty'. Here are just a few shadowbox ideas to get you started:

- Just cut out a scrap of that old wedding dress and frame it in a shadowbox with a picture of the bride and groom along with the wedding announcement or the newspaper clipping announcing their engagement
- Frame a grade card along with a photo of the loved one as a child and include a miniature of their favorite toy or interest
- Frame a letter and include miniatures that represent the story of that person's life

Quilts

As I sorted through my grandmother's stores of fabric, I came across a small quilt top—crib-size, with alternating pink and white blocks. Embroidered on each white block was a kitten playing with a ball of yarn. My mother was the only girl, sandwiched between two boys, so I wondered if this was supposed to be for her and that my grandmother simply never got around to finishing it in time.

I decided to finish that little quilt top and I gave to my mother as a gift for Christmas. A few years later, my mother gifted it back to me just in time for my second daughter's birth. To this day we still use the quilt each night to tuck my daughter in.

If you are unfamiliar with quilting, that's not a problem, there are actually companies that specialize in making quilts out of used clothes or fabric, according to your specifications. A quick internet search for 'memory quilts' will yield plenty of companies to contact. Here are a few ideas to get you started on that memory quilt:

- Use old clothes or fabric (the less elastic or stretchy, the better)
- Scan photos and have them printed on quilt fabric

- Use fabric scraps or notions (ribbon, lace, rickrack, etc.) to embellish a quilt
- Write a story on the back with indelible marker telling the story of the person's life

Scrapbooks

Assemble a scrapbook with a few of their personal papers which help tell a story about that person's life. There are so many scrapbooking sites on the internet, and scrapbooking supplies at craft stores that I'm not going to go into much detail on this subject. A stop by your local public library will also yield a cornucopia of books and design ideas to help you preserve your loved ones memories.

You Are Not Alone

"You aren't alone. There is such a degree of shame that accompanies this and I hate to see that. Because every person goes through a time in their life when they can't be organized—loss, divorce, illness..." Excerpt from appearance on KCUR radio, the Walt Bodine Show, March 2008

I meet clients who are stressed out and deeply embarrassed by the state of their homes. They are reluctant to have even a professional organizer see the mess or step around the piles of clutter.

But if you were to stand in my shoes, you would see the growing trend—we have overscheduled and overworked ourselves into an exhausted (physical and mental) state. It naturally follows that our homes will suffer too, from our busy lifestyles.

Overworked Americans

In the United States, Americans work an average of 25% hours more than Europeans and have only twelve (versus an average of 28 days off in Europe) vacation days per year. The U.S. Labor Department reports that, in 57 percent of married couples, both the husbands and wives work.

With that much work and so little time off, it can be difficult to be organized.

The Cult of Speed

"When you accelerate things that should not be accelerated, when you forget how to slow down, there is a price to pay."
—Carl Honoré, "In Praise of Slowness"

Later in this chapter, I will discuss Economy of Movement and encourage you to conserve your energy while multiplying your efficiency. Please don't confuse this—I don't expect you to move faster, simply more efficiently.

Carl Honore has written two profoundly insightful books—"In Praise of Slowness" and "Under Pressure," that I recommend you read. We must strike a balance between speed and efficiency and between taxing our bodies and minds to the breaking point and accomplishing nothing at all.

We are overextended in debt, time and mental resources. Most of us are exhausted at the end of each workday, yet we still need to find time for our families and friends. Is it any wonder we feel overwhelmed or find ourselves stressed out? So we go out and we shop or we eat, to compensate for the stress in our lives.

I believe there are fundamental flaws in how we exist as a society, which help contribute to a vast amount of our clutter. Unfortunately, we don't have the time or the resources to address those issues. As much as I would like to fix the world or at least the state of our country today, even I have my limits!

So you see—you aren't alone, you aren't an oddity. You are just another person who woke up one day and realized that something needs to change. So, are you ready for a change? Turn the page and we will discuss some tips on how to get started!

Organizing Tips and Advice

"Our first game is called 'well begun is half done.'"—From the movie "Mary Poppins." 1964

Before you begin the actual organizing process, you need to be prepared. There is nothing more frustrating than starting on a task and getting distracted or realizing that you don't have what you need, when and where you need it.

In this chapter I will give you tips on:

- finding organizing opportunities in the midst of your day-to-day life
- what materials and supplies you will need
- guidelines for the decision-making process
- different organizing methods
- finding help in your organizing quest
- how to avoid simply shuffling your stuff around
- making the most of your organizing sessions

By the time you are finished with this chapter you will be rarin' to get organized!

Create the Time

"For every minute spent in organizing, an hour is earned." —Unknown

An often-repeated phrase I hear from clients and class participants alike is, "I just don't have the time." It is used as an excuse for the current state of clutter in their homes and also as an excuse not to take action.

Becoming organized and clutter free, does not take as much time as you might think. In fact, it creates time by simplifying your life. How many times during the day could you find one minute, or even five minutes to organize?

When I buzz into my kitchen in the morning, my husband moves to the side and stays out of my way. In less than five minutes, I have cooked an egg, toasted a slice of bread, brewed coffee, wiped down the counters while I waited for things to cook and lined up my daily vitamins at my spot at the kitchen table. I've also put away all of the items (except for the pan I used to cook the egg) that I had out for making breakfast. My coffee is poured and creamer has been added before I sit down to breakfast. After I finish eating, I stand up, put my chair back into place, rinse off the plate and load the dishwasher. I'm in and out of the kitchen in less than fifteen minutes and I have left it clean and ready to use for preparing dinner in the evening.—*Time spent organizing/cleaning: 3 minutes*

I make a point of not letting clutter take over my car by remembering to grab a bag and load it up with any trash. I take it with me when I get out of the car and throw it away in the nearest garbage can. —*Time spent organizing/cleaning: 30 seconds*

When I brush my teeth in the evening, I pick up any bottles, cans or brushes and put them away in the proper place. —*Time spent organizing/cleaning: less than 30 seconds*

In my office, before I begin to write or check email, I have to turn on my computer (I turn it off at night to save electricity). While I am waiting for it to boot, I make a short list of things I need to work on for the day, stack any books up and out of the way, put my pens and desk supplies away and take a quick look at my Inbox. —*Time spent organizing/cleaning: less than 2 minutes*

I think you begin to see what I mean. There are many opportunities just like those I have described above, where we sit and do nothing – zone out and waste time. If those moments are spent organizing, that's less organizing you have to do later. Time you could spend with your spouse or children.

In reality we spend a good deal of our day waiting for something. Here are some tips on things you can do while you are waiting...

While you are:

- Waiting for the waitress to bring your lunch order—clean out your purse
- Waiting for the water to heat for your shower—tidy your bathroom sink
- Waiting for your dinner to heat in the microwave—clear off your kitchen table
- Waiting for the commercials to end—begin sorting through your stacks of papers
- Heading in the door from work—hang up your coat and purse in the closet

Carve out even more time to organize by:

- Checking the news online just once a day
- Limit checking your emails to just twice or three times per day, maximum
- Wake up ten minutes earlier, even if you simply sit and sip your coffee—we can all use some quiet time in the morning

to collect our thoughts
- Combine trips (use the pharmacy at your local grocery store and shop while your prescriptions are being filled)

These are just a few ideas. The point is, the time is there, you just need to learn how to utilize it more effectively. Any time you find yourself waiting for something to happen, you have been given golden moments to incrementally organize another aspect of your life.

You need to make a conscious choice to change aspects of your lifestyle—these changes will help you to be more organized and I will talk in detail about them in Part 3. For now, I want you to think about what you do each day and ask yourself as you move through your day, "What can I do, at this very moment, to be more organized?"

Let your eyes fall to just one item and pick it up and put it away. Now do it again with another item and another. The time you were sure you didn't have will double and triple, until you find yourself organizing as you are moving about with your daily activities.

So what do you need so you can organize effectively?
You need to:

- Have a few basic organizing materials and supplies
- Be physically and emotionally ready to organize
- Understand the two basic organizing methods
- Be ready to follow a couple of rules

Materials and Supplies

"I am so happy with how my master bedroom looks, but I have just one complaint. I didn't get to go shopping for any organizing supplies!"—Client feedback after an organizing session

You don't need much to get started. In fact, the less you have to go and find, the quicker you can begin. Here is your basic list:

- Black Sharpie or permanent marker
- Ballpoint pen
- A spiral-bound notebook or legal pad
- 3-5 garbage bags
- 2-3 boxes
- Scotch tape

In other words, a shopping trip to Crate and Barrel is *not* in order. My clients are often surprised at such a short list and many of them make an earnest effort to convince me that what they *really* need is a new cabinet or organizing hardware for their closet, etc. Unless the space is barren of furniture or storage options—a rare thing indeed—I strongly advise against purchasing anything not on the list above.

One client in particular pops into mind. We were tackling her kitchen and she had already sold herself on the idea of buying a cabinet and putting it *on her back porch* to store pots and pans in! We both live in the Midwest, where the temperatures can fluctuate by 115 degrees (-10° in winter to 105° in summer) throughout the year. We are also plagued with these creepy insects called June bugs (yes, they actually do appear in June) as well as a myriad of other insects. I had this sudden horrible vision of her finding a wasp's nest inside her frying pan one fine summer day.

I looked her in the eye and said firmly, "You have all the room you need within your existing kitchen cabinets—we just need to make sense of them and then you will find more room inside than you ever thought you had." She was doubtful, but by the time we finished for the day, we *did* find the room. All of those pots and pans found a lovely home inside an easily accessed cabinet inside her kitchen—right next to the stove and right where they belonged.

My point is you don't need expensive organizing solutions. They promise the world, or at least tell you they will make you organized now and forever—and they don't deliver. Stick to the basics, it will save you money and a good deal of hassle.

Take out your permanent marker and tear several pieces of paper from your notebook. If you are tackling a mountain of paperwork, make the following signs:

- Trash
- Shred
- ASAP—Pay/Do/Call
- File

If you are going through possessions other than paperwork, prepare the following signs:

- Trash
- Stays Here
- Goes Elsewhere (elsewhere in house, car or office)
- Donate
- Sell

Tape each sign to either a trash bag or box, depending upon the size and shape of the item and space your 'piles' far enough apart that you can, a) easily reach them and b) they won't end up mixing together.

Keep your notebook within arm's reach. You will need your notebook and a ballpoint pen before you begin to organize each room.

If you are dealing with a significant amount of clutter and don't have the room for these piles—take a moment and make room by moving belongings out of your way as much as possible. Eventually, you will be able to tackle that mess as well, but first you need room to work!

Keep, Toss, Donate or Sell?

Sometimes it is very clear what needs to go in the trash, be kept, donated or sold. Other times, the way is not clear, which is often a contributing factor to clutter. If you have a difficult time making decisions, your clutter accumulates until it overtakes your living areas.

Here are some guidelines to help you determine whether you should keep, toss, donate or sell an item. Begin by asking yourself:

- Am I currently using it?
- Is it in prime operating condition?
- Do I have multiples of this item?

You should keep an item if you are using it on a regular basis and you have it in the appropriate place (kitchen items in kitchen, bathroom items in bathroom, etc.)

Once you have decided an item must go, you need to determine the best method of disposal.

When you should donate an item:

- You haven't used this item in more than one year
- It can be used by someone else in its current condition
- Clothing for example, once washed (missing buttons and small tears are acceptable to donate, many thrift store shoppers are happy to replace buttons or mend if it means a cheaper price)
- You don't have the time or energy to post it for sale and follow up on it and dicker price with a buyer

When you should dispose of or recycle an item:

- The item is broken and has not been repaired

- The item is a consumable (food, medication, etc.) that has expired
- Has no practical use (there is a limit on how much bric-a-brac you can put on your shelves)

When you should sell an item:

- You are willing to invest time and energy in speaking/dealing with buyers
- You know of a good consignment store or are familiar with eBay or Craig's List or have had success holding garage sales

The Two Methods

There are two main methods you need to choose between when tackling your clutter. The first is what I call the Drawer by Drawer method and the second is the Four Box Five method.

Drawer by Drawer

I recommend this method if you have a small clutter problem. For example, if the top of your dresser is messy or your home office doesn't have a decent filing system, the drawer by drawer method works quite well. In most cases, clients who use this technique have low clutter and it is simply a matter of streamlining their filing system or increasing the efficiency of existing storage space.

You literally start by working through one drawer at a time. As with all organizing, start out small and gradually increase the chunks of organizing you do. Don't half-complete the task and then wander off and start another one. Finish the project at hand and expand out, one drawer or closet at a time.

Four Box Five

The Four Box Five method is designed specifically for extreme clutter situations. It focuses your attention on the main issue, regaining living space. If you used to have a couch which is now buried beneath clothing and boxes and papers or if you can't walk into rooms because they are so full of stuff—this is the method for you. You will need four boxes, possibly five.

Label your boxes as follows:

- Goes Elsewhere
- Remains Here
- ASAP!!
- Trash/Shred

Isolate one area. We will use the missing couch as an example. Begin uncovering the couch, one item at a time, putting everything you pick up into one of the four boxes.

Goes Elsewhere should hold items that belong in other parts of house or even items to be donated.

Remains Here only applies if you actually intend to keep the object you picked up right in this very spot. Since we are using a couch as an example, a pillow or throw might be a Remains Here item.

ASAP is just what it means—deal with this right away. Put any bills you might find into this box. Anything that goes into this box must be dealt with and filed or paid or called on etc., within the next 48 hours. If it isn't important enough for that kind of response, than it doesn't belong in the box.

Trash is self-explanatory.

Shred - If you wish to shred any paperwork, I advise having a separate trash bag—labeled Shred—next to the Trash box.

Friends, Family or a Professional?

"A friend of mine told me he would be happy to come over and help me get organized. He said, 'You will have to be okay with me playing Hitler.' I wasn't, so he didn't come over!"—Client comment during organizing session

If you are a chronically disorganized person, you have probably come to realize that the act of organizing is not something you do well when you are by yourself. Frequently, simply having another person in the room with you helps you to remain focused and continue organizing. Here are some questions to help you decide if that person should be a friend or a professional organizer.

Working with a Friend or Family Member

- Do you know what to do, but need someone present who will help you stay focused on your goal?
- Are they patient and non-judgmental?
- Do you work well with them?
- Will they be objective and not try to impose their own idea of "being organized" on you?
- Do they have the time to see you through the project and not leave you with a mess?

If you answered "yes" to these questions, a friend or family member might be able to help you get organized. Working with another person may be especially helpful to complete an organizing project you have begun on your own or with the help of a professional organizer.

Hiring a Professional Organizer

- Are you unsure as to where or how to begin organizing?
- Do you need to learn organizing systems and techniques?

- Do you have a deadline for completing your organizing project (such as an impending move)?
- Do you need the expertise of someone trained in helping chronically disorganized people?
- Are you dealing with medical, physical and/or psychological issues in addition to disorganization?
- Will you need ongoing organizing assistance or maintenance?
- Do you need someone to help you organize large quantities of things or papers?
- Do you want or need the objectivity of a neutral third-party?

If you answered "yes" to some or all of these questions, you will greatly benefit from the assistance of a professional organizer who is skilled in working with chronically disorganized people.

No Churning Back!

A conversation between a client and me during an organizing session:

Me: *"I noticed that you just placed that paper in the 'go elsewhere' pile? Where does it need to go?"*

Client: *"Oh, this paper? Well, I want to read it later and make sure I don't need it. I also need to write down a date that is listed on it."*

Me: *"If it is an important paper than it needs to be addressed right away, why don't you put it in the ASAP pile?"*

Client: *"Well it isn't really that important; I just don't know when I'll get to it."*

I would like to address a trap that you can easily fall into when organizing. I like to call it 'churning.' The conversation box above is a good example of churning—the act of moving an item from one pile to another (or leaving it in the same pile) without any real plan of what to do with it. Churning happens when we aren't paying close enough attention to the 'rules' of the game. If the 'game' is getting organized, then churning is the equivalent of moving back two spaces on the board.

Pick up an item and try to remember to only handle it once.

- Where does it need to go?
- Is this paper really important?
- Do you have a use for this item right now?
- Are there duplicates of this elsewhere?

Make a clear, strong decision right now and put it in the appropriate pile. Don't over-think it. Now move on to the next item and the next and the next.

Often, I find that clients begin to churn unconsciously. They do this most often when they are tired. They have been making decision after decision after decision and now they are exhausted! Remember to take frequent breaks, drink plenty of water, get up and stretch and walk around.

It takes a lot of energy at the beginning of the organizing process. The frustration and anxiety we have felt over the clutter has already dulled us, but as more and more areas of your life become organized it will be less taxing. I'll talk about this more in Energy Begets Energy. In the beginning of your organizing, be kind to yourself and take breaks when you start to churn. It will get easier, I promise!

Economy of Movement—Part I

A very important technique to use while organizing is Economy of Movement. The idea of it is simple—each movement that we make should be as efficient as possible.

The seeds to this idea started in one of my first jobs. I was a teenager working in the mail room for an investment firm. I helped collate, insert and mail prospectuses to potential clients, ran errands and did general clean-up. Collating is pretty mindless work, and I liked it because it allowed me to talk or think on subjects or a variety of other activities that I wouldn't have been able to do while performing a more challenging task. But it was boring, so I tried to think up ways of getting it done sooner—despite the fact that that meant less pay—so that I could then pursue whatever new subject had caught my interest. After all, I was just thirteen; my attention span in the 'work' department could be rather... err... *spotty*.

I began to see how many steps I could eliminate—steps to the copier, steps to the paper trays, the supplies and the postage machine. Conversely I realized I couldn't overload the paper trays or stack the envelopes too high, or the resulting collapse, paper jams and mess would make the task even longer. I began to count every stack, find the 'perfect' number and would then spout it off to the nearest co-worker, whether they wished to hear it or not.

Thus was born the idea of Economy of Movement which I have continued to use in different forms throughout my life. If I've lost you, you think I'm really weird, or you are wondering if I'm going to start spouting off numbers—relax and continue to read. It gets better, I promise!

When you wash and dry a load of laundry, all that is left is to fold and put the clothing away, right? Okay, now as you are standing there, maybe with the television on to keep you entertained, do you fold a shirt and then immediately put it away? Or do you make a stack of like items (your son's clothes in one pile or separate stacks of shirts, pants, etc.) and then put them away?

Hopefully you answered "yes" to the latter. If not, stop what you are doing, you're wasting valuable time and effort! Folding clothes, separating them into stacks or categories and then putting them away is an example of Economy of Movement, plain and simple.

Practice Economy of Movement by staging items into the piles (boxes or bags) that I listed under 'Materials and Supplies,' which prepares them to go to other locations. Once you have sorted through the area you want organized and you have made your piles, *then* you can leave the area and deliver each stack to its appropriate location. Using this approach means that you, a) don't leave the area that you are organizing and get distracted by other clutter, and b) conserve your energy to move the items you have organized and get them put away in their appropriate 'homes.'

It takes a little practice and perseverance to effectively utilize Economy of Movement. Some may find it easy, but most will slip up and find themselves in another room wondering what they were doing. Keep thinking Economy of Movement and pretty soon you will find that you get more accomplished in a chunk of time than you thought possible. And in this busy world of ours, you will find that to be a welcome trait to have.

Energy Begets Energy

Getting organized takes time. After all, the clutter didn't appear overnight and it definitely isn't going to go away with the snap of your fingers. Oh, how I wish that nose twitchy thing that Samantha on *Bewitched* did actually worked for me! However, you will find that as you accomplish your goals—first the small ones and then ever-larger challenges—your energy levels will grow and grow. Energy truly does beget energy! Each success gives us hope and empowers us to reach out and change even more.

Although I found myself organizing at an early age, I have still had times when I allowed paperwork or possessions to take over my life. I got distracted and busy, things piled up and when it reached 'critical mass' I would do something about it. Usually my organizing was accompanied by a rant on how "I can't stand this mess a second longer!"

A few years ago that rant hit as I pawed through my tiny sink drawer looking for eyeliner. A pair of tiny, sharp tweezers impaled one finger and drew blood. I looked down at the drawer and realized it was time for a change. The small space was a mess. I had makeup, hair pins, clippers and tweezers all jumbled together with hair and dust and even a few Band-Aids thrown in for good measure. What a disaster!

I pulled out a box of varying sizes of plastic Glad Ware containers and took it back to my bathroom, where I sorted the contents of the drawer into piles (hair care, makeup, manicure tools, etc.) and then placed them into appropriate-sized plastic containers and arranged them back in my drawer. Three years later, everything is still in place and easy to find. Clearly defining the area by sorting the items into categories meant that it was easy to keep that level of organization up. I was so energized that I tackled the mess under the bathroom sink the next weekend and the entire master closet the weekend after that.

Often my clients have lived so long with the mess that they are simply overwhelmed and don't know where to start. They stare around at the mess and feel their energy drop just by the act of looking at it! A little jump-start is just what we need to get organized.

Some Final Tips

Not too long ago, I conducted an organizing session with the mother of two young girls, aged six and eight. The girls had so many toys and games that even I was overwhelmed! They were very friendly and outgoing and asked questions about everything. I ended up enlisting their help in sorting through their possessions and found that they had an easier time parting with their belongings than their mother did.

There was very little indecision on their part, they either wanted to keep it or didn't and were very clear about their wishes. I had secretly feared involving them, worrying that they would want to keep everything, but it was obvious that they, even more than their mother, wanted the area to be less cluttered, so that they would have more room to play. In the end, the kids were the experts on what they played with and what they didn't—so it was essential we had them with us for the decision-making process.

Organizing can be hard work and having some extra help on your side makes a big difference. So ask everyone to pitch in—your kids, spouse and even your friends.

So how do you get that energy to tackle the organizational challenges in front of you?

- Be well rested before you begin
- Have a bottle of water nearby to stay hydrated and eat a high-protein meal before you begin (protein will give you energy and help you stay alert for all of that decision-making!)
- If you are a parent, ask for help from others in babysitting your children, so that you can devote your full attention to the task at hand
- Enlist the help of family or friends or a professional organizer
- Start out small and build up (one room, even one drawer, at a time)

- Practice Economy of Movement
- Reward yourself. (No, not by buying more items! Instead go out to dinner or see a movie after you have accomplished an organizing task)

So...are you ready to start organizing? Great! Let's get started!

Section 2: Let's Get Organized!

Visualize Whirled Peas

"I don't know *what to do with it. That's your job,* you're *the organizer!"*—A client's response when asked what she wanted to see happen with a cluttered spare bedroom

To effectively organize, you have to begin with some kind of vision of what you want your space to be. It isn't enough to say, "The room's a mess, I have to clean it up" and it doesn't help to bring in someone else and say to them, "Make it better," without some kind of guidelines or willingness to make it happen.

I once worked with a client whose family had given her an ultimatum—"clear out these closets or else" and she was unhappy and mad at the world. In particular, she was directing her anger towards me since her family was regrettably absent during this remarkably 'un-fun' organizing session. Nothing I said was right and she seemed determined to take offense where none was intended. It was an uncomfortable three hours, I can tell you!

I am going to assume that this is *not* the case with you. My hope is that you are reading this book with an open mind, wanting a change and believing that it is possible. As a professional organizer and through my ongoing training to become a life coach, I believe that each of us has unlimited potential for change and growth. To be a part of that process, one that helps effect a lasting change in an individual's life, is one of the main reasons I do what I do. So, if you still aren't ready to get organized, I hope that I can help you change your mind before you finish this book!

I spent the first section of the book talking about how the clutter worms its way into our lives and gave you techniques on how to begin to deal with it. Now I want you to do just one more thing before we begin organizing each space—visualize world peace.

Your home is, or should be, your safe little world. It is a place where you go to find comfort, peace and rest. That is our goal here. You should be able to come home and de-stress from the outside world and enjoy your haven, whether you rent an apartment or own a rambling home.

So for the rest of this book I want you to visualize the home you want to have and *believe* that you can have it. As you go through each room of your house, close your eyes and imagine what it can be, what you want it to be.

Most of us don't have the means to buy multi-million dollar mansions, but we can make our spaces, such as they are, into oases of calm. We have the ability, each of us, to make our little worlds peaceful and tranquil. And to do this, we need to take one room or space at a time.

If you have not already done so, now is the time to identify the room or space in which you wish to begin. Is it your kitchen or your bedroom? Is it a gloomy basement—full of boxes—that you would like to see converted into an exercise room? Or perhaps your garage is the pressing issue; do you want it empty of all that furniture, so you can park your car in it?

Even if it is as simple as a dresser or a closet—identify it, pull out your notebook and write it down at the top of a blank page. Now close your eyes and visualize what this room will look like when you are done. Got it? Okay, now answer the following:

1. What do you want to happen in this space?
2. What function or functions should this space have?
3. What is it being used for now?
4. What is working and what isn't working?
5. Finish this sentence: "This space will be perfect once ."

What Works For You?

I worked with a client who had limited space in her cramped older home. Her living room was the room she targeted as needing the most help. Her toddler's toys had not only taken over the living room, but were inaccessible in many cases and a hazard in others. There were toys on the floor, toys on the couch and all of the bins she had purchased a few months ago were stuffed full of everything from infant to toddler appropriate toys. Balanced precariously on the television were stacks of DVDs.

There is no 'one size fits all' system for organizing. This case was no exception. When I asked the client if she would consider relocating her child's toys to the little girl's bedroom, the client gave a very persuasive argument for the child's toys remaining in the living room. This was the room where the client and her husband sat down and relaxed after a long day away from each other and the client did not want her daughter to be isolated from them and have to play with her toys alone in her room. For the client and her husband, removing all of the toys would not be the optimal solution. So instead of moving all of the toys out of sight, we sorted through them, separating the toys into five categories:

- Stuffed animals—to go into crib
- Outside toys—to go out to back yard
- Outgrown/unused toys—which were put in a "to donate" bag
- Toys to stay

Once we knew which toys stayed, we could make a decision on what we might need in terms of furniture or shelving to hold them. As it turned out, the set of three canvas toy bins adequately held the 'toys to stay' with room to spare.

The DVDs were alphabetized and placed in a drawer below the television that had been used to hold a farm's worth of stuffed animals. As we placed the stuffed toys in the child's crib, her mother made the decision to cut that number in half and arranged the 'nicer' stuffed toys on the top of a bookshelf.

I advised her to make a couple of lifestyle changes as well. At the close of the evening, she and her husband would make a game with their daughter of putting away her toys, incorporating it into the bedtime ritual of bathing, tooth brushing and reading a book. I also advised the client to go through the toys once every six months and rotate toys from the bottom of the bins to the top or remove items that were outgrown, broken or unused.

Since the client used a computer at home daily, she scheduled a 'recurring task' in her calendar program to remind her to do that task at regular intervals in the future. At last report, she, her husband and their daughter were all enjoying their organized living room and had incorporated the suggested changes into their routines easily and successfully.

Take your time with this. It is very important that you have a clear picture of what use (or uses) this space will be devoted to. Include your family members in this process as well. Ask them what they want to see happen with the space (this also encourages them to participate in helping you clean it up!) and whether they have needs different from yours.

I mention this because I learned my lesson the hard way. I was working with a client early on in my organizing career and I neglected to get input from the husband on what he wanted from a basement family room. We were halfway through packing away most of the trophies and collectibles that cluttered every inch of the fireplace mantle when he returned home. He was horrified to see his prized possessions being removed, a crisis that was neatly averted by my engaging him to install shelving on an unused wall. Whew!

By taking the time before you organize to visualize what you want with the space and take into account others' wishes and needs, you are now ready to tackle the most intimidating spaces. Take that vision, write it down and keep it firmly in hand. It is time to move through the various spaces in your house and *get organized*!

Room by Room

We have talked about it long enough and it is now time to start organizing! You should now have:

- Organizing materials ready to go
- Notes on your first room or space to organize
- Some water or liquid refreshment close by
- Comfortable clothes and shoes and be well rested

You have it all and you are ready to start organizing. You know what room or space you are going to tackle first and have everything you need to begin. Here are some specific ideas and tips for each room. You may wish to do a quick review before starting on the room or you may wish to just leave the book open to the applicable spot—either way... Happy Organizing!

Living Rooms and Family Rooms

"What works for you and your family? Go with that. Don't worry about what others think. If you are okay with your children's toys being in the family room, go for it. We don't live in a 1950s perfect house, and really, who would want to?!"—My response to a "Let's Get Organized" class participant

As 'public space,' living rooms and family rooms often serve a variety of interests. Formal living rooms are easy to organize, in comparison to informal living rooms and family rooms, because the space is by nature 'formal' and, therefore, less cluttered.

If you have an informal space, it is quite naturally a gathering space for the entire family, as well as guests. No matter how small this space is, it should be a place of comfort and evoke a sense of relaxation and home.

That is why clutter can be such a mood-killer here. After a long day, you head for your living room or family room to relax and watch a movie, play a game with the kids or work on some crafts while listening to music. If you don't have the opportunity to sit down on a couch without toys poking you in the back or shoes tripping you as you walk in, you are not going to feel relaxed.

So how do we make this better? First we have to define what you need (for comfort, tasks, etc.) and create special areas for these needs. We also need to maximize storage space, get all of those DVDs and CDs in order and sort through the rest of the clutter.

Define What You Need

So what do you want when you look around your living room or family room?

- What are the activities/functions currently performed in this room?

- Are there any activities/functions that should be moved elsewhere?
- Is this a formal living room, a place to display your finest antiques and art?
- Is this the place for a home computer?
- Do you need a crafts/scrapbooking station here?
- Do you need a special play area for the kids?

We each have individual needs for our shared living areas. For example, in my living room, we have a couch, television and room on a bookshelf for my toddler's books and some toys. We keep the DVDs near the television for ease of access as well as some books on interior decorating and gardening below the DVDs. Other than a few knickknacks, that is all we have in this small, cozy space.

Create Special Areas

Perhaps you want to use this room for general family entertainment, which includes watching television, working on the family computer and board games. Try creating clearly defined areas for each. Group books together, use a closet or cabinet to store games in one place. Put the kids' art center at a table in the corner. Consider having one basket per child for toys, so that the room isn't overrun.

Maximize Storage Space

Although I often roll my eyes and carry on about the organizing solution industry—there are some very effective products for organizing your living areas. If at all possible, I recommend built-in storage solutions throughout your house. They now sell a variety of ottomans that double as storage (remove the top and access the box inside) and are fabulous for storing games or blankets for when the weather turns cold.

If you have any of those decorative boxes and trunks, remember that they can and should be used to store things. If you like candles, keep a store of tapers in a tall container. They are out of the way until you need one. If you like potpourri, keep your fresh potpourri wrapped up in a different box nearby, ready to change out once the displayed potpourri loses its scent.

Consider moving family pictures to walls instead of displaying them on surfaces. It makes them easier to dust and leaves the surfaces clear.

Managing Media

Many families, these days, have large collections of DVDs and videotapes. As long as you still have a working VCR, keep those videotapes. If you don't have a working VCR, it's time to get rid of them! You can transfer videotapes into digital form with the right kind of hookups to your computer. Type 'video tape to DVD' into a search engine on the internet to find out how to do it or to find services that will do this for you. Having your home movies and favorite Disney movies off of videotape and into digital form will save you a good deal of space in your living area It also prevents further deterioration (VHS tapes have a limited lifespan and are quite sensitive to light and heat).

Go through each item and make sure you want to keep it. If you haven't watched a particular movie in a long time, consider getting rid of it. If you are certain you wish to keep it, set a 'watch by' date on it or sit down and enjoy it! Consider alphabetizing by title, or grouping by genre (children's, action, sci-fi, etc.).

If you still have vinyl records, audiotapes, or even 8-tracks—consider having these transferred to digital form as well, then sell or donate the original items in order to take up less space. If you still have too many items and not enough storage space, you will have to start making some hard decisions on what will stay and what will go. Remember, you only have a limited amount of space and you deserve a clutter-free life—making these decisions can improve your quality of life far more significantly than if these items were to stay.

Sort It Out

Shoes, clothes, hats, dishes—none of these items belong in the living room. Place them, and any other items that do not belong in the living room, in the 'Goes Elsewhere' box. If you find trash or items to be donated, place them in separate boxes or bags, taking care not to leave the living room until you have completely sorted through everything.

At the end of your organizing session, you must take the 'Goes Elsewhere' box away and distribute its contents to the appropriate locations. Even if those destinations are cluttered and messy in their own right, you still need to take the items there. Remember, grouping 'like with like' is essential to maintaining an organized space!

At this point your living room is clear and organized. However, I have one last suggestion for you.

If you take your meals in the living room instead of at a table in the kitchen or dining room, please consider making a change. Even if you live alone, sitting down at the table and eating can be far healthier for you away from the television. Studies have shown that adults are likely to consume an average of 15% more calories at a sitting, when distracted by the television than they would if the television were turned off. So flip off the television, sit down at your kitchen table and enjoy a meal together. And if the kitchen table is too messy to eat at, well, let's talk about organizing kitchens next!

Kitchens

"No chaos, no creation. Evidence: the kitchen at mealtime." -
Mason Cooley

Where our bedrooms should bring us comfort at the close of each evening and leave us feeling refreshed each morning, our kitchens should rejuvenate us in the morning. They are the spice and the soul of our home even if you aren't a gourmet chef and your microwave and toaster see more use than your stove or oven ever will.

After a long day of work, my husband and I are sometimes too tired or unmotivated to clean up. We eat dinner and walk away, plates still on the table and pans and dishes covering the counters. This is rare, but it sometimes happens. When I walk into my kitchen the following morning and see the mess I find that, no matter how hungry I am, I cannot eat until I have cleared the dirty dishes and wiped down the counters. I have made it a rule that before cooking can begin, the surfaces must be clear. I feel so much better since I decided to do this—I feel less harried and stressed and cooking becomes a far more pleasant experience.

Most of my clients complain about not having enough space in their kitchens. It seems that there are too few counters, overly full cabinets and never enough drawers or pantry space for everything. In every organizing session I have had with a client where the focus fell on a kitchen, I have found that they truly *did* have enough space for everything—it just took some re-thinking of the space available to us.

Numbering high on my list of 'get rid of' are the bread machines, espresso machines, banana racks, slow cookers, fondue pots and woks. These are followed closely by all those darned gadgets we seem to accumulate: egg slicers, pastry brushes, and cookie cutters (when is the last time you made cookies with cookie cutters?!).

Okay, I'll admit it. I had two can openers in my kitchen for the longest time—one was electric and only I seemed to be able to finagle it into working right. My husband refused to use it and instead he used the manual can opener, which I despise. Eventually the electric opener broke and we found a manual can opener we could both live with. And earl on we did get rid of the hot oil fryer (in the rare times we need to fry something, we have pots and frying pans that work just fine), the bread machine and also a wok that wouldn't work with our glass-top stove.

So how do we get our kitchens whipped into shape?

- Group like items together
- Remove all unnecessary items from your counter
- Store items safely
- Sort it out
- Adhere to food expiration guidelines
- Grow it yourself
- Label it

This sounds like a lot, but one step at a time, right? Let's start with...

"Some sensible person once remarked that you spend the whole of your life either in your bed or in your shoes. Having done the best you can by shoes and bed, devote all the time and resources at your disposal to the building up of a fine kitchen. It will be, as it should be, the most comforting and comfortable room in the house."—Elizabeth David (1913-1992) French Country Cooking

Group like items together
Inside of those cabinets lurk the strangest of combinations—salt is nestled next to canned string beans, crackers share space with dishes.

That container of raisins you were eating the other day ended up with the cans of baby corn. It's time to group like with like.

We aren't just talking canned goods here; I mean *everything* from your cookware to your gadgets and all of the food in between. I was organizing a client's kitchen and we found flour in *three* different spots in her kitchen! In another client's kitchen it looked as if a large bottle of vinegar had spawned and given birth to several smaller bottles and don't get me started on the untold numbers of spices.

If you group like items with other like items and then designate specific zones for them, you will find that cooking in your kitchen becomes a breeze. You will also spend far less time searching for ingredients or battling the cans and boxes and bags stored willy-nilly inside your cabinets and shelves.

<u>Remove all unnecessary items from your counters</u>

No matter how little you cook each day, having your counters covered with stuff is simply not acceptable. It is stressful to try and work around when we do want to cook. Even putting together a sandwich can be a pain if you don't have a clear surface.

We also have a tendency to accumulate a different contraption for every little need. I am devoted to my rice steamer, for example. We use it up to three times a week, so it stays on our counters. I also drink coffee every day, so the coffeemaker is there as well. But how many items on your counters are used infrequently at best or perhaps never? We have limited space on our counters and if you find you don't have room to cook or prepare a meal, then take a hard look around at each of the objects on your counters and ask yourself the following:

- *How often do I use this?* —If you aren't using it at least 2-3 times per week, you should consider moving it.
- *Do I use it at all?* —Unless it has decorative value (and keep these to a minimum), put it somewhere else or get rid of it.
- *Do I have more than one of this item?* —I once had a client

who had three different toasters—one was broken, one didn't handle bagels and the third one was the one she used every day. I advised she donate the first two to charity since she could use the bagel toaster for toasting regular toast just as easily as bagels.

- *Is this in the place that works best for my needs?* —If you have your rice steamer at the opposite end of your kitchen from the sink or your spice rack out of easy reach of the stove, re-think the locations.

Clear your counters and watch your stress levels go down significantly. Having the space to prepare your food and access your outlets and appliances will make all the difference in the world!

<u>Store Items Safely</u>

This may seem like a no-brainer, but there's a little story behind this one.

A few years ago I bought my husband an odd birthday present—a thirty pound box of Lemonheads candy. He was ecstatic. Personally, every time I smell Lemonheads it reminds me of lemon Pledge, and who would want to eat furniture polish? But my husband absolutely loves them and ate a handful each night for several months.

They sat on the floor of our pantry and were gradually reduced to a box of about ten pounds over months of snacking. One fateful day, our deep fryer, which we had foolishly located on the *top* shelf of the pantry, seemingly decided to leap to its death. It landed in the open box of Lemonheads and soaked them in old, rancid oil. Thank goodness *we* didn't get hit by this suicidal deep fryer!

My husband was so angry he threw away the fryer along with the ruined box of Lemonheads. To this day we have still not purchased a deep fryer due to the bad memories associated with them. For that my waistline is grateful! However, it was a good lesson as well:

- Keep the heavy items down low and the lighter items up high—this reduces the chance of a heavy item falling on you.
- Don't stack cans more than two cans high
- Make sure that items that need to be refrigerated or frozen are in their proper spots—read labels, often they indicate an item should be refrigerated after opening.

Storing items safely and at the appropriate height will prevent most kitchen accidents.

<u>Sort It Out</u>

I know your plastic containers are a mess – admit it! How often do you reach inside that cabinet or drawer and try to pull out a matching container and lid to store your leftovers in? How often do you find what you are looking for on the first try?

Find some space, hunker down and sort your plasticwares...

- Sort by size (square, round, etc.)
- Match each container with a lid
- Throw out (or donate) containers that you don't use, are ill-fitting, or damaged

Now you can re-introduce the plasticwares into their storage space, keeping lids with containers for easy location when you need them!

Adhere to food expiration guidelines

When organizing your kitchen remember that even 'non-perishable' foods go bad. Nowadays, nearly all food we buy has expiration dates clearly listed on the package. By paying attention to those dates, you can adjust your meals to incorporate those foods into your diet, well before their expiration date. Here are some guidelines to consider when deciding whether to keep or dispose of the food in your pantry:

- canned foods (2-5 years)
- cereal (6 months)
- pasta (1 year)
- spices (6-12 months)
- flours (3-6 months)
- grains and legumes (1 year)
- dried herbs (6 months)
- condiments (1 year)

Many of my clients or class participants groan over the spices and herb expiration guidelines. I can understand this all too well. I remember when I bought my house nearly nine years ago. I went out to the store and bought every spice from A to Z, so that I would "always have whatever I needed." A few years later, a significant outlay of money went straight into the trash can, many of the spices had never been opened.

This is one reason that I counsel most of my clients to avoid buying in bulk. Unless you are buying an item that you and your family tear through on a timely basis, it simply is not a good deal if it expires before you have used one-quarter of it.

Grow it yourself

And on the subject of herbs, may I suggest planting a garden? If you live in an apartment or townhouse, you can put together a small herb garden near a window in a pot and grow your own. Here in the Midwest, I grow the following herbs:

- common sage is available for harvesting year round (fabulous wrapped with prosciutto around tilapia and sautéed in olive oil and pepper)
- basil (this annual often re-seeds itself)
- horehound (dried, it makes a soothing tea for sore throats)
- thyme (great for chicken recipes and it produces leaves available for picking nine months of the year)
- rosemary (I buy several plants each spring; this herb is fabulous for chicken recipes and homemade breads and pizza crusts)
- marjoram (good in meat recipes)
- parsley (great flavor for soups and salads—grown from seed each year)
- Spearmint (any variety of mint grows well here, but watch out, they can take over!)

I find that fresh herbs taste far better. A short trip out the back door adds amazing taste and aroma to any dish for just a few cents! Your shelves aren't taken up with untold numbers of bottles either.

Label it!

Organize your canned/boxed/bagged non-perishable foods in your pantry or cabinets by category. It makes putting your food away after a trip to the grocery store so much easier to find—now and later! In my own pantry I have items categorized and labeled in following manner:

- Breakfast items
- Pitchers/containers & Drink mixes
  - Beans
  - Soups
  - Pastas
  - Sauces
- Fruits
- Tomato products (sauce, diced, chopped)
- Stir fry fixings (we love our stir fry!)
- Olives & Misc Vegetables
  - Baking/dessert
  - Box dinners

Depending on your own individual needs, how you categorize your pantry will probably be different than how I would. Consider the list above to be a starting point to laying out a pantry that works best for you.

Thanks to having labels in place in my pantry, my husband can easily put away groceries in the same order as I do—this reduces the chances of us 'losing' items and then buying too many. We can easily find items and make sure that we aren't overspending on groceries or not eating perishables before they expire.

Another good idea is to make your labels adjustable if possible. Our food needs change, and if the labels are adjustable, you can simply move them to a more appropriate location as your storage needs shrink or expand. Here is a picture of my pantry ten years ago...

As you will see, I used large metal clips. These were easily adjustable to any changes in the future, which I needed since the labels were up and easily bent and knocked over.

Here is another photo of my pantry in my new house. Our needs have changed in some ways, and so my labels have changed as well...

And one more photo...

If you wish to, by all means find classier ways to label and organize your pantry. For me, and for many of my clients, the pantry is constantly changing and evolving. By using the labels we can easily sort the incoming groceries into the correct location.

Maximize Your Storage

I recently saw a kitchen that had cabinets with the pull-out shelves. These are a relatively inexpensive item you can buy at a home improvement store and install yourself. Instead of reaching way back into the cabinet, you just pull on the shelf and the item in the very back slides out to an accessible point. Fabulous!

Add hooks for coffee mugs to the bottoms of your cabinets, but be sure to leave room for your small appliances.

Take a stroll through the organizational section of your local Target, Wal-Mart or Bed, Bath & Beyond and learn about new ways to stack your plates, organize your spices or utilize a lazy Susan in a tight corner cabinet.

<u>Clear the Kitchen Table</u>

Growing up, I remember that we always ate dinner at the table. This was a time to come together after a long day apart. And although we weren't a "Leave It To Beaver" family—the conversation would inevitably turn to homework and the fact that I hadn't completed it—having that time together was important.

Clear off your kitchen table and use it for its intended purpose. This can be a constant struggle for many of us. Often the table becomes a catch-all as we arrive home from work or a staging area for various tasks. In my house, I still catch myself depositing items there.

Take the time to clear it of all clutter, wipe it down, lay down clean placemats and place a scented candle or a floral arrangement in the middle. Relax and enjoy a meal together as a family, with the television off. After a day spent organizing your kitchen, you have earned it!

Kitchens are usually the second room in the house that we find ourselves in, first thing in the morning. So let's turn our attention now to the space we need organized when we are still bleary-eyed with sleep—our bathrooms.

Bathrooms

To properly organize your bathroom, you need to cull any items that are not being used, clear your surfaces, sort your items into categories and maximize your available storage space.

Start by doing the following tasks:

- Make a stack of items you use daily—scout around for an organizer that will allow you to store them more effectively
- Ensure that all medications are out of the reach of children (even if you don't have any young children, you may have grandchildren or friend's children who visit occasionally)
- Remove multiples (curling irons for example) or unused items and put them in a 'donate/sell' pile
- Dispose of or donate (if they can be fixed) any items that are not working (an electric razor, for example)
- Pack duplicates of toiletries in your suitcase

Discard items as follows:

- make-up, hair products and lotions you haven't used in 6 months
- products that are dried up or evaporated
- prescription medications that have expired

- over-the-counter medications you haven't used in 6 months
- old razors, scissors or other dull and rusty metal items

Clear Surfaces

Just like with kitchen counters, bathroom counters should only hold what you use regularly. Move items off the counters into medicine cabinets and out of your way. Now you can easily access the sink and any outlet.

I cannot emphasize enough, how important it can be to have a clear surface to work with—even in a bathroom. This is one of the first rooms we spend time in immediately after waking and it can set the tone for the rest of your day.

For years, I allowed my sink to be cluttered with items. It made it nearly impossible to clean—I would spend ten minutes clearing off the sink to clean it and another ten minutes wiping down all the items to put back on the clean sink. It also drove me crazy every time I knocked something down trying to reach a lotion bottle or had to pull stray hairs off of my toothbrush. We finally purchased some under-the-sink totes, organized our two tiny sink drawers, and installed a medicine cabinet instead of just the flat mirror on the wall. Our sink surface is now clear and easy to keep neat and clean.

<u>Sort it Out</u>

Purchase buckets or caddies, clearly label them and separate your 'under the sink' toiletries into categories. Under our sink, we have the following categories:

- Cough and Cold (this could also include Tums or Pepto Bismol)
- Hair products (extra brushes, combs, gels, sprays, etc.)
- First Aid
- Skin Care (topical ointments, sunscreen, lotions)
- Analgesics (aspirin, Tylenol)

Some of these items have migrated to our medicine cabinet. I regularly re-assess what is in our medicine cabinet and move items down to the below-sink totes if we have stopped using them. Sunscreen is a good example. During the warm months we use it constantly, so it makes more sense to have it in the medicine cabinet within easy reach.

During the winter months it will go into the skin care tote under the sink.

Maximize Space

If extra space is needed, consider installing a medicine cabinet if you don't already have one. The same pull-out shelving that I suggested for the kitchen can also work under the sink in a bathroom cabinet. It allows you to reach items stored all the way at the back of the cabinet with little or no fuss.

Re-Purpose Items

Re-purpose items for easy storage solutions. We throw so many empty containers away each day in this country. But many of them can be re-used in another form. My grandmother was well known in our family for her re-purposing of boxes and containers. She would cover the box with scraps of matching wallpaper to make it more decorative. A tin can would become a handy receptacle for makeup brushes. The empty shoebox would hold small bottles and containers underneath her sink.

Look around your own home and envision those empty containers in a whole new way. An empty quart-sized milk container with the top cut off, could hold tall, lightweight objects easily and a former laundry soap box could serve as an under-the-sink tote.

Bathrooms are an essential part of our daily routine. Having yours in ship-shape condition means less frustration in the morning when you are still blinking the sleep out of your eyes. As you move about your morning routine, you will inevitably find yourself in your closet, wondering what to wear, so that is where we will go next!

Closets

"Please all and you will please none." – Aesop

What I am going to say next is not popular—especially with my female readers. But I'm going to say it anyway, because it is real, and it is good advice. And also because Aesop was correct, you can't please everyone.

So here goes...

I've been in homes where every closet was jam-packed full of clothing, shoes and accessories. Homes in which clothing is hung haphazardly from every doorway and boxes and stacks tumble into hallways, threatening to reach out and trip you as you pass by. Nearly every one of my clients swear to me that yes, they wear it all, every bit of it. Ladies (and gentlemen), I have seen it all and unless you are a quick-change artist and change your outfits at least five times a day—every day—*there's no way you need that many clothes.*

Get rid of those stacks of shoes. Divest yourself of those multiple pairs of black pants, shirts in every color and matching handbags in every shade and go back to basics. You are not Imelda Marcos and yes, the deal you are getting on that pair of pumps really should be passed up.

See what I mean? Unpopular.

I am here to tell you that if you want change, if you want to re-make your home into the haven that it should be—that you deserve it to be—you have to change your shopping habits. You have to make some difficult decisions on what is *really* important in your life. Is your stuff number one? Or is your sanity and the happiness of your loved ones more important?

It all comes down to numbers:

- Square footage in house devoted to storage
- Number of days in a week, weeks in a month, months in a year

Get out your tape measure and measure your closets. Add up all the areas and write the square footage down. This is the amount of space you have to store your things.

Period.

Unless you are willing to give up square footage outside those areas—and doing so will impede you in your goal of being organized—then this is the amount of space you should limit yourself to.

No matter what the closet and storage solution manufacturers try and tell you—sooner or later you have to accept that if you don't have the space to store the items, then it is time to *let them go*.

So how do we start reducing the amount of stuff in our closets? It isn't going to be an easy journey, but we will review the 80/20 Rule, the 3 E's and then take clothing closets and linen closets in turn.

80/20 Rule

Most of us wear 20% of our clothes 80% of the time. When I first heard that, I was shocked. But when you think about it, it makes sense. So why are we keeping so many extra clothes? It's time to figure out what we wear, how often we wear it and then reduce, *reduce*, reduce!

One of my clients found that, yes, the 80/20 rule was true—the kicker was, she was wearing clothing she didn't like! 80% of the time! As we sorted through her closet she discovered clothing she had forgotten about, tried on some of the outfits, and decided to radically change what she was wearing and get rid of the clothes she hated. When I checked in on her two months later, she reported that she had received several positive comments on her outfits.

The 3 E's - Evaluate, Examine and Eradicate

First we need to 'Evaluate' what is in our closets—how big of a mess is it? 'Examine' our reasons for keeping the particular items and then 'Eradicate' any items we no longer need nor have used.

Go through your closets once every six months. Put it in your day timer, on your calendar or schedule it as a task in your computer date book—any way you like to remember, but just do it.

Get rid of it...

- If you can't remember the last time you wore it
- If that button or zipper is still busted, or the hem or seam has come loose

- If you have had it for more than a year and it still has its tags
- If it doesn't fit you right now and hasn't for longer than you can remember
- If it is outdated, not your style, or just the wrong color for you
- There's dust on the top of hanger or on the item itself (come on, you know it's been sitting there *way* too long if it's collecting dust!)

Clothing Closets

In 2007 I marched into my closet and decided I had had enough of wrestling with my clothing. I was tired of constantly having to shove aside all of the clothes that didn't fit, weren't my style or that just didn't work. Hours later, and several large bags of clothing stacked outside, my closet looked empty and desolate. All that was left were the items I could wear *right now*—the pants and tops I liked and wanted to wear and my sharply reduced shoe collection. In comparison, my husband's section of the closet looked positively full.

A year later, I hadn't missed any of the clothes I removed. Ten years later, I get by with half the space I used to have (our "new" 1899 Victorian has limited closet space).

I also managed to shed an armful more of clothing by reversing my hangers, yielding even more empty space in the months that followed. Here are some specific tips for organizing your clothing closet:

Clothing:

- Reverse hangers (hook from the back of the pole forward) on the pole for all of your clothing. After you wear an item, replace it on a hanger facing the right way. At the end of six months or a year, remove all the clothing from hangers still facing the wrong way and place it in your donate or sell bag.
- If you haven't worn an item in more than two years, ask yourself "Is keeping this item worth the space it takes up in

my closet?"

- Group like items together (dresses with other dresses, for example)

Shoes:

- If you haven't worn them in over a year, get rid of them
- Weed out multiples—do you *really* need five pairs of running shoes or three pairs of gardening shoes? Seriously now!
- Remove old/worn/out of date shoes and donate to charity (keep your feet healthy and well-supported!)

Linen Closets

I have a tiny linen closet in my hall. Due to its small size, and the bad lighting, I need the space to be well-organized and easy to access. I first decided what I wanted to keep in the closet and then separated them into stacks by category. I then made labels for the categories: twin sheet sets, full sheet sets, extra pillowcases, Kleenex, light bulbs, blankets. Then I placed the labels on the shelf below each stack. This helps my husband (and me!) to put any freshly laundered items back in their correct location. As you are organizing your linen closet, remember to:

- Organize all towels by size:
  - Bath towels
  - Hand towels
  - Washcloths
  - Remove old/worn/out of date towels and donate to charity or rip up and use as rags
- Organize your sheets into:
  - Sets for each size of bed (twin, double, queen or king)
  - Pillowcases (regular, king size)
  - Remove all incomplete sets
  - If you have flannel sheets put them on top, if it is winter, or on the bottom below the cotton sheets, if it is summer for ease in accessibility.
  - Remove old/worn/out of date sheets and donate to charity

Finding clothing and linens in your closets will now become much easier. Your guests will be able to locate the spare towels or sheets and you won't have to shuffle through a mass of ill-fitting clothing to find the perfect outfit. With some of the core areas out of the way, I would like to turn your attention to rooms that need just as much help as our main living areas... our children's rooms.

Children's Rooms/Play Areas

"I take a very practical view of raising children. I put a sign in each of their rooms: 'Checkout Time is 18 years.'"—Erma Bombeck

Just as the master bedroom is our personal sanctuary, so should our children's rooms be for them. Here is where they can go to get away from us and our nagging and rules and general adult grumpiness. You know it's true, even as we need a break from our kids, *they* need a break from *us*!

Children's rooms are usually the smallest living spaces in the entire house, yet they are a major hub of activity and use. Our children sleep, play, study, create and bring friends over to these small spaces. What items we put in them and how we arrange them can be very important.

Think outside the box on this. Could the closet become a reading nook? Can you double a seating area with a hinged-lid storage box? Think about putting a bookshelf at the head of the bed for nighttime reading pleasure or consider installing shelving on walls to display art or model cars.

Most importantly, kids need room to move around, a place to spread out a bit and play. They also need to learn basic organizational skills—it will help them in a variety of ways (from succeeding in an office job to turning in their term papers on time). If they learn good habits now, our children can carry them into adulthood and become organized, effective adults.

So how can we create a place of rest and relaxation, play and study—all in one room? Read on to find out...

Create Different Spaces

So what goes on in kids' rooms? Sleeping, playing and school work—right? If your son or daughter is lucky enough to have a second room devoted to playing, it makes the actual bedroom setup even easier.

No matter whether we are dealing with one room or two, the premise is the same; there should be separate spaces for each main activity. After all, you don't want them distracted with toys when they need to do homework or sleeping when they could be playing.

Well, okay, the second example was intentionally silly, but you get the idea. Having areas in their rooms designed especially for their activities and interests will give your children a place they can call their own.

As I guide you through organizing your children's playroom and bedroom I encourage you to involve your children in the process. From sorting to labeling, incorporating organizing solutions and encouraging a standard of neatness, your son or daughter will learn much-needed organizational skills. These skills will benefit them for years to come.

<u>Visualize the Space</u>

So what are your child's interests? What gets them interested and keeps them coming back for more? Model cars? Games? Books?

Before you can even begin organizing your child's space, you have to have a vision for what the space will become.

My older daughter was always very creative—she wrote stories, drew pictures and loved to paint. She was a voracious reader, so a bookshelf was definitely in order, as was a desk for her art and writing. A bulletin board on the wall above her desk gave her space to pin her latest creation. In later years, she used the bulletin board to hold her notes on stories and also for her favorite quotes.

A television was far less important than the space to write and draw. Knowing this about my daughter helped me to assist her in organizing her room in the most efficient manner possible.

<u>Sort It Out</u>

Begin by sorting your child's possessions into categories. I'm sure you will come up with others, but here is a list to use as a starting point:

- Stuffed Animals
- Clothing and shoes
- Art supplies
- School (backpack, projects, homework, etc.)
- Books
- Hobbies (model cars, collectible Barbie, etc.)

Label It!

Before my daughter could read I cut out pictures of toys and labeled her toy bins. This helped her in the sorting process (stuffed animals, art supplies, books, etc.) Later that morphed into teaching her to read simple words.

Add Organizing Solutions

Each child should have a clothes hamper and be reminded to use it for their dirty clothes. This encourages a basic standard of neatness, which I will discuss in more detail in a moment. Over-the-door pocket shoe organizers are perfect for holding shoes, hair clips and a variety of small toys. If possible, label these pockets to avoid their becoming catch-alls.

Toy boxes can be convenient methods of storing toys, especially since you can also sit on them. There are also chairs with hinged seats and tables with hinged lids. Consider using some of these to keep art supplies neatly put away when not in use.

If you or your spouse is handy with wood, consider installing a built-in window seat with either a hinged lid or shelving below. Your son or daughter can enjoy a book or sit by the window drawing on a rainy day and built-in storage is always my number one suggestion to my organizing clients!

Enforce (and model) A Standard of Neatness

Bottom line, this means that *your* room needs to be clean. Sorry moms and dads, but you can't expect your children to be neat and tidy if you aren't!

I am a big believer in teaching our children responsibility and I taught my daughter how to clean her room in a rather odd way. I would regularly come in and pick up each and *every* item off of the floor and then dump it on her bed. This way, she had to at least move the stuff off of the bed before she could sleep in it. I would then vacuum the floor and tell her to go through everything and put it in its proper place.

For a long time that required my constant presence and direction in her room. Kids aren't born knowing how to organize, so it helps to teach them early how to pick up and put away their toys and belongings in some semblance of order. It doesn't have to be a stressful, crack the whip, 'get your room organized or else' scenario. This can also be a good time to talk with your kids about school or friends or your plans for the weekend.

While you are there in the room with them, encourage your child to group 'like' things together and have distinct categories. If they become distracted or lose focus, redirect them gently yet firmly back to the task at hand.

Limit Toys

Another unpopular piece of advice (second only to limiting the number of shoes and clothing we own) is the idea of limiting the amount of toys our children have or are given. As a generation born in the full swing of American consumerism, the idea of limiting or even [gasp] *reducing* the number of possessions we give to our children, is tantamount to child neglect for some parents.

Well folks, take a long look at some of these children who have gotten everything and then some, how are they turning out? Are they up to their eyeballs in debt before they hit age 25? Are they caught in the loop of having it all, right now, the hottest, the raciest, and the 'OMG, I gotta have it right now' orgy of acquisition?

Unless you are Warren Buffett, or some mega billionaire like Bill Gates, you aren't doing your children any favors by getting them the latest and greatest in every color of the rainbow, you just aren't. And even if you are a mega billionaire, you still aren't doing them any favors by giving them so much.

Limit your big purchases (a bicycle, a trampoline, etc.) to ONE per birthday or holiday. Find out what your kids want more than anything and then buy what is reasonable to you not them. For instance, my older daughter asked for a Barbie car (one that she could get in and drive) for Christmas one year. Considering that we were living in a one-bedroom apartment with little room for storage and no real good places for her to drive it, AND the fact that I couldn't afford it, meant that she didn't get it. Fifteen years later, when asked, said she didn't mind *too* badly not getting the Barbie car!

Childhood is a wonderful, magical time full of learning experiences and love. The best way we can show love for our children is by spending time with them, talking with them, including them in our daily activities and listening to (and encouraging) their dreams. The latest Xbox game or kid's cell phone are poor substitutes for our physical and emotional presence in their daily lives.

Evaluate Regularly

Children grow up way too fast. I know all about it from personal experience. At the publishing of this book, my oldest will turn twenty and my second child is nearly two. I can personally attest that twenty years came and went in what seems like a few heartbeats and the two years since my youngest was born have flashed by in the blink of an eye.

As children change, so do their interests. Yesterday's Dora the Explorer is replaced with today's Build-A-Bear. Baby Einstein and Sesame Street give way to Lego's and Wheelies.

So mark your calendar and re-visit your children's rooms every six months (at least) and weed out clothing that is outgrown or that your children have no intention of wearing. You know which outfits I mean, no matter how cute that pair of corduroy pants look, if you hear, "Mommm, I CAN'T wear that, everyone thinks I look like a dork," then let the pants go. You aren't going to win that battle.

Gather up all of those Happy Meal toys and if your child protests, let them give a good argument for keeping them. Then set a reasonable limit on how many they can keep. If you both agree on five, for example, then if she gets toy #6, one of the others (or the new one) will have to go in the donate bag.

Go through everything and weed out anything that is broken, needs batteries, is borrowed from a friend, etc. Do this with your child and *be firm*. This helps you to keep your organizing skills tightly in tune and it teaches your kids how to make decisions and stick to them.

Please Donate

All of those clothes and shoes and toys and books that your kids don't want—they need to go to new homes. Donate them to your favorite charity and give yourself a big pat on the back, not only are you getting a tax write-off but you are giving someone else the opportunity to make good use of clothes and toys they often can't afford.

Years ago, a parent I knew casually mentioned that when their children had outgrown their clothes they simply *threw them away*.

Name brand clothes like Gap, Carter's and Oshkosh—and they weren't in bad shape at all! I was horrified at the thought of all of those perfectly good clothes ending up in a landfill.

Even if you have never shopped at a local used clothing store or consignment store, please rest assured that there are many, many people out there who can and will happily use second-hand clothing, toys, books and an endless array of other household items. Not only are they happy to get such a good bargain, in many cases finances dictate that they either buy second-hand or do without. Donating is a win-win, and it teaches your kids to think of others and to recycle.

Children's rooms are challenging yet fun. I always enjoyed figuring out how to make a special place for my daughter to work on her artwork and feel comfortable each night. Take your time with this room; it is one of the most important rooms you will ever organize. And speaking of important rooms, were you wondering when I would address the master bedroom? Wonder no longer, here it is...

Master Bedroom

"Clutter can definitely push the love out of a relationship. If there is clutter and disorganization in this most intimate of spaces, is it any wonder that the passion has diminished in your relationship?" – Peter Walsh, "It's All Too Much"

Just as children should have their own rooms to escape from us, so the master bedroom serves as an escape from the rest of the house and its occupants. At least, it should be.

Look around your bedroom—what do you see? If you have clothes to fold, shoes scattered on the floor—if you have clutter on the surface of every piece of furniture in your room—if your dresser drawers are stuffed so full you can't even close them...

Well, that's a good reason to be holding this book right now. Remember, you deserve a sanctuary, not bedlam!

So what we need to discuss first is what function your bedroom provides. I believe it has three functions:

- Sleep
- Lovemaking
- Escape

I think those are pretty self-explanatory. In each case, having clutter significantly limits your ability to do any of those functions. You cannot properly relax when clutter covers every surface, or you trip over piles of stuff on the floor. And you can't, well, *you know*, when clothing is piled on the bed.

Some professional organizers will tell you that you shouldn't have a television in your bedroom. Personally, I think that is a decision that should be made on an individual basis. I have a television in my bedroom, but it doesn't see much use. It definitely comes in handy

103

if my husband wants to watch one program and I want to watch another—one of us stays in the living room and the other relaxes in the bedroom.

Remove What Doesn't Belong

Eating a late-night snack in bed isn't the awful no-no it once was. But leaving the dirty dishes stacked on your furniture for days on end can be rather [ahem] *off-putting*.

Ditto for removing anything else in your room that doesn't belong there—children's toys are a good example.

Remove Excess & Clear Surfaces

I truly admire the ability of those who can live with little or no furniture—minimalists seem to have the least problems with clutter. I am not a minimalist; instead my motto often seems to be, "I'll *make* it fit!" So at regular intervals, I walk through my house and re-evaluate what is within each room and earnestly attempt to reduce the furniture population.

The same can be said for knickknacks. Regularly go through your room and reduce the knickknacks to a reasonable level. Reasonable level is individual-specific—but the rule of thumb for my own decisions is, "Can I dust it regularly without it being a hassle?" Keep that in mind as you work on each piece of furniture in turn.

Organizing Your Dresser

Dressers don't need to be messy, so why are they inevitably a jumble of clothing bulging out of the drawers?

I only keep the current season in my dresser at any one time. In the fall I pull all of the shorts and short-sleeved shirts out and replace them with pants, long-sleeved shirts and sweaters. I also regularly re-evaluate them, as I do so, I remove any items I haven't worn during the season and I place them straight in a 'donate' bag. Remember to categorize your clothing—shirts in one drawer, pants in another and intimates in a third. If you have plenty of room as I do in my dresser then you can split your items into more specific categories—tank tops, bras, pantyhose, etc.—into separate drawers.

Model Good Behavior

I mentioned this in the Children's Rooms section, but it bears repeating.

- Make your bed every day
- Toss your dirty clothes into a hamper not onto the floor
- Tidy up a little each day

I'll admit it, making the bed each day is still something I struggle with. But it feels wonderful when I do. I love coming into my bedroom after a long day and pulling the covers down and slipping in between them. If you don't normally make your bed, try it for a week and see if it works for you.

I found that both my husband and I had a bad habit of just leaving our clothing wherever we had been standing at the moment we stripped them off. In our close quarters (our bedroom is only 12' by 12') having piles of clothing or shoes lying around was unacceptable—especially after tripping several times! It doesn't take any effort to toss your clothes into a hamper at the end of the day.

It takes only minimal effort to keep your room tidy once you have finished organizing. Depending on whether you are a morning person or a night owl, take a couple of moments each day to pick up. I usually find a stray dryer sheet (from folding clothes on our bed) or clothing tags lying around. I also take the opportunity to give the furniture a quick swipe with a microfiber cloth and remove any accumulated dust.

And that's about it. Now let us address one of the most dreaded of tasks—paperwork.

Home Offices and Paperwork

"Information is a source of learning. But unless it is organized, processed, and available to the right people in a format for decision making, it is a burden, not a benefit."—William Pollard

Paperwork, paperwork and more paperwork! Whether your home office is a small desk located in the kitchen, a niche carved out of closet or hall space, or a full room devoted to your home business—it is essential to your sanity that you be able to have some kind of organizational system in place.

- Do you have a special place for your incoming mail to go?
- What about a drawer where you keep all of your receipts?
- Do you know where your stapler, tape, stamps, paperclips and blank envelopes are at all times?
- And what do you do with all of those bills and statements with your personal data on them?

In this section we will address what to do with all of those stacks, sorting techniques, guidelines for keeping financial records, processing mail (including magazines and catalogs) and setting up a filing system, along with other invaluable tips.

Paperwork doesn't have to be a monster headache. Employing even some of the strategies that follow will reduce your stress levels and ensure that you keep the important papers and get rid of the rest. Let's get started, it is high time to get it all sorted out.

"I do not take a single newspaper, nor read one a month, and I feel myself infinitely the happier for it."—Thomas Jefferson

Stacks and stacks and STACKS!

In every class I teach, I hear the same thing repeated over and over—"I don't know what to do with all of the paperwork and mail I receive. It just piles up and there is so much of it!"

Did you know that *one issue* of the New York Times contains more information than the average person living in the 17th century would receive in an *entire lifetime*? Even if you manage to escape the 'buy, buy, buy' mentality of our nation, you will find that the information pipeline is already set at overflow and quickly approaching flood stage.

Folks, there is only so much information that you can read, listen to or watch in a day before your brain says "enough!" Continuing to try and set aside papers or magazines to be read 'when you have time' is simply *not* going to work. Review it now or set a 'to be read by date.' If the day comes and goes without you having read it, donate the paper or the magazine to charity and try to be kind with yourself. Personally, I think Thomas Jefferson gave some incredibly sage advice (see box above) that you may wish to take to heart.

We only have so much time in each day and often we have to make hard decisions on what we will choose to read and learn and when we need to walk away and enjoy our lives. You need to find that balance and move on or end up buried beneath a mountain of papers—literally and figuratively.

The mental alarm bells begin to ring each time I work with a client who says, "I can't throw this away yet. I need to read it, try to remember it." There are many variations on this theme:

- It's related to a medical condition they have
- Their friend or family member or spouse needs to look at it and deal with it
- It's a catalog they *may* want to buy from
- It's a bill or a legal document or a 'to-do' that is long overdue

And so on and so on.

Just as with your other possessions, you need to make some hard decisions. You cannot let paperwork take over your living space. If it already has, then it is time to reclaim your life.

<u>Sorting It All Out</u>

Remember 'Four Box Five' I spoke of in Section One? It's time to put it in action. You will need enough room on your floor for the following categories:

- File
- Trash/Recycle
- Shred
- ASAP!!

Let's review each of these in order.

File—Recently paid utility bills, medical explanation of benefits and any current information that has been processed and/or paid can all be filed away.

Trash/Recycle—Magazines and catalogs you have finished looking through or aren't going to be looked through. Anything you don't need to shred. Pick your destination and put them in!

Shred—Papers that contain personal information (name, social security number, etc.) or any papers you may wish to use as shredded mulch.

ASAP—Anything that needs to be paid or dealt with immediately. This includes any magazines that have been piling up! Set read-by dates for the magazines and catalogs by attaching post-its and then discard (or recycle) after that time has elapsed.

Remember to deal with each of these stacks. It isn't enough to simply make stacks, once you have gone through everything you need to then do the filing, the shredding, recycling or shredding and go through your ASAP pile right away!

Receipts

For more information on what receipts to toss and what to keep in your files, please read all about it under Advanced Organization—Organizing Your Finances.

Paperwork—Keep or Toss?

The following is a guideline for the different personal files you should maintain and keep. I advise each individual to have a file cabinet in their home with clearly labeled tabs and folders. If you have been simply stacking paperwork and thinking you will 'file it later,' STOP! File it now! Take the time to purchase manila folders, labels, hanging file folders and a metal file cabinet (more sturdy than plastic). Keep all of your files in one place for ease in locating and then file them alphanumerically.

- <u>Taxes</u>: Keep all tax files for seven years and then purge (unless you own a home business). Anything prior to that can be shredded, but business records need to be kept indefinitely.
- <u>Utility Bills</u>: 3 months (or not at all if you can access this information online)
- <u>Credit Card statements</u>
    - ◦ Active credit cards: 3 months (or not at all if you can access the information online)
    - ◦ Closed accounts: Create a file labeled "Closed Accounts"
- <u>Medical bills/Explanation of benefits</u>: 6 months OR as long as needed in case of accident or litigation
- <u>Legal documents</u>—as long as is applicable
    - ◦ Child custody agreement: as long as child is under the age of 25
    - ◦ Divorce agreements: Permanently, in case of questions in regards to titles to your home or personal possessions come up
- <u>Pay stubs</u>: 12 months
- <u>Automobiles:</u> for as long as you own the vehicle—this should include all receipts for repairs, oil changes and the title to the vehicle. In the event of a sale, you will have all the documentation for the next owner to have.

- Bank Statements: 3 months, unless you own a home business. I usually keep only one year's worth of business banking statements in my main files and store any of the rest in my archived files for ease of reference.
- Insurance: As long as particular insurance is active. For monthly statements, 6 months is all you need, but for the information regarding co-pays or locations of providers, keep these unless a new book is issued.

If you use financial software such as Quicken, then you don't even need to keep your utility bills or credit card statements past the previous month after you have reviewed them for any errors or suspicious transactions. We will discuss these software programs in more detail later in Advanced Organization.

Processing Mail

I get a large stack of mail each day and I actually enjoy receiving it—even if a large percentage of it seems to be 'hate mail' (bills). For many years, I would sit down each day and go through each piece of my mail, one at a time. However, I found that dealing with my mail on a daily basis (sorting it, opening it, sending payments, etc.) was far too time-consuming. Between checking my bank balance, reviewing our household budget and sorting through each piece of mail, I was spending 20-30 minutes *each day* processing mail!

I decided it was time for a change and I now have a basket for incoming mail. Each day I pick it up from the mailbox, quickly shuffle through it and look for any 'love mail' (checks, letters, cards) and then deposit the rest into my Incoming Mail basket. Then once a week (usually Sunday afternoon when it is quiet and my husband can handle watching our toddler) I go through each piece of mail, reconciling bills, entering payments into online banking and tossing junk mail and the paper refuse into the 'Shred' basket.

All in all it takes me 45 minutes to an hour to process all of my paperwork for the week. It then takes me another 20 minutes to shred everything and spread it in my yard (part of my composting 'no weeds' technique). By processing mail once per week instead of daily, I saved myself at least *seven* hours of paperwork processing each month.

I personally recommend that you process your mail at least once per week. While it used to be that you would receive your bills with at least 30 days lead time to pay them, it now can be as little as 14 days. Waiting longer than once per week could jeopardize your good credit and also incur late fees if you miss payment dates.

Now let us address the problem of the many and varied magazines and catalogs we find ourselves deluged with:

Magazines:

- Limit yourself to a maximum subscription of two monthly magazines
- Limit buildup by disposing of any more than the past two issues
- Keep them in one location, nice and neat
- Recycle them by donating them to a charity or putting them in the recycle bins marked 'magazines'

Catalogs:

- Go through these immediately, order from them if you like, but *do not* keep them to 'look through later.' If you don't have time once a week, then you don't have time at all
- Recycle by putting them in the recycle bins marked 'magazines' or shred them and use them in your garden as weed block.
- Opt out of receiving those catalogs by calling their 800 numbers and requesting that they stop sending you their catalogs. Most companies will appreciate your call, since they

are investing money and postage into each of those catalogs with the hopes you will buy something. If you aren't interested in purchasing their products, you are saving them money with that phone call!

Now that you have your papers in order...

Purchase (and use!) a Paper Shredder

Reduce the amount of paperwork you throw away by purchasing a paper shredder. You can find a basic strip shredder for under $30.00 at a variety of stores including Wal-Mart, Office Max, Target or Office Depot. I purchased a heavy duty cross-cut shredder for $180 and it can shred up to twenty pages at a time, as well as credit cards. I shred everything, including envelopes, junk mail; even catalogs (feed them in a few pages at a time). I then add the shredded paper to my compost heap and also in my raised garden beds to smother weeds.

Top Reasons for purchasing a cross-cut paper shredder:

- Reduces amount of trash going to landfill
- Reduces chances of identity theft (strip shredders shred everything into long strips, whereas cross-cut shredders make it nearly impossible for someone to ever piece together financial information and steal your identity)
- Can be used for compost in your garden (the birds love it add it their nests as well)
- Quick and efficient

You have gone through your paperwork, sorted through your mail and shredded a stack of papers you no longer needed. Now about that 'File' stack...

Setting Up A Filing System

If you don't already have one, I strongly recommend that you purchase a steel file cabinet. For most people, a two-drawer file cabinet will be perfect for your filing needs. If you own a business you may want to consider a 4-drawer file cabinet (or more if you have a large number of client files). I am able to comfortably fit my active files for my two businesses and all of our personal files, inside of a 4-drawer file cabinet. I use the top drawer for my organizing business, the second drawer for my housecleaning business, with the third for all of my personal files and the bottom drawer has my archived files (closed accounts, inactive clients, etc.).

I have included a list (see box) of exactly how I have set up my personal/family files. Every person's situation is different, so just view this list as a starting off point. The tabs for the hanging folders are in all caps and the individual file folders are in lower-case:

AUTOMOBILES

[YEAR Make Model]

BANK ACCOUNTS

Bank – Checking - 1234 (last 4 digits of acct #)

BILLS

CREDIT CARD

Chase – 1234 (last 4 digits of acct #)

LOANS

Nelnet – Student Loan – 1234 (last 4 digits of acct #)

UTILITIES

Electric Company

Time Warner (Cable, Internet, Digital Phone)

Water Company

INSURANCE – Auto, Home & Life

State Farm – 2006 Honda Civic

State Farm – 36204 Hight Avenue

INSURANCE – (Medical)

EOB's (Explanation of Benefits)

Provider Information (provider directory, listing of benefits)

MISCELLANEOUS

Community Center

Rebate Offers/Tracking

Receipts (big ticket items)

MORTGAGE

Mortgage Statements

Purchase paperwork

PERSONAL INFO

[Your Name] – Birth Certificate, Passport, Immunizations

[Your Name] – Credit Reports

[Your Name] – Pay Stubs

[Your Name] – Resumes/Work History/Recommendations

[Your Name] – School/Education

PETS

Vaccination Paperwork

Vet Visits/Receipts

RETIREMENT

401k

Investment Information

Money Market Account

Roth IRA

TAXES

2008 Taxes

2007 Taxes

Property Taxes

APPLIANCES*

Appliances – Basement

Appliances – Garage and Yard

Appliances – Living Areas

*I place the Appliances folders at the back of my files because I rarely access these. There is no need for them to take up room in the front when you aren't going to be accessing them regularly. These folders contain all of the manuals and paperwork that comes with our appliances (television, refrigerator, etc.) and they add up quickly, so I broke them down into the three categories for ease of access.

Another nice way to keep your files in order is to color-code them. Office supply stores sell manila folders and hanging files in a variety of colors. This makes it even easier for you to file your paperwork or find it again later. I suggest using the following color coding system:

Green = Income (Bank accounts, 401k, Money Market, etc.)

Red = Bills (credit cards, loans and utilities)

Yellow = Personal Information (work, school, etc.)

Blue = Insurance (home, medical/dental, auto, life)

Pink = Assets (house paperwork, household appliances, etc.)

Note: I do NOT color code. The reason for this is simple – if I run out of a certain color, I'm not stopped in my tracks from creating a new folder or label. I stick the plain old boring manila folders – simple, easy to use, and I never run out.

This completes the organizing of your core living areas. Many of us are challenged by the less-frequented areas of our homes. The next chapter, "Organizing Your Other Spaces," will address these areas in detail.

| Page

Organizing Your Other Spaces

In the previous section we covered our main living spaces. These are the areas we see, have access to and live in each day—but what about those *other* spaces? Basements and attics, garages and storage sheds can become the worst catch-all areas, because if we don't see them every day, we tend to forget about them.

If your garage has become filled to the point that it is no longer used as a house for your cars or your basement is a maze of boxes and stacks of furniture, then let us focus our attention on these areas now. Even if we do not actively live in or visit these areas on a daily basis, it is important to know what we have stored in them and then we can decide whether the space could be better used for something else.

In our own basement, we finally took the plunge and began to finish it out. We have decided that we want to use the space for the following purposes:

- Guest bedroom/craft room
- Library/reading area
- Laundry area
- Play room/Exercise room

Our house is not large; therefore, every inch of living space is valuable to us. When our basement project is complete, it will be a place for me to curl up with a book while the laundry cycles and our daughter plays with her toys.

Now if I can only convince my husband that we can raise the roof and put on a second story on the house...master suite here I come!

Basements and Attics

Walt Bodine: *"So tell me about an area of the house that you don't look forward to organizing."*

Me: *"Well, sometimes basements and attics can be a bit...icky...lots of dust and spiders! But I've learned to deal with it all."*—Excerpt from KCUR's The Walt Bodine Show, March 2008

So what is in your basement or attic? Boxes upon boxes of stuff? Broken furniture? Untold numbers of projects that you plan on getting to someday?

Basements and attics are often like closets, only on a bigger scale. We open up the door and toss the items in and promise ourselves or our spouse that we will get to it later.

The problem is this—tomorrow comes far too quickly on the heels of yesterday. The project that you meant to complete two years ago, still sits in a box, accumulating dust and 'someday' never comes. When you look at an item, a piece of furniture or that awful knickknack that your great-aunt Vera gave you—and you can't decide what to do with it, you put it away in the basement or attic for that improbable 'someday.' But if you don't know what to do with it today, chances are you never will.

So where to start?

To properly organize a basement or attic you need to first make space for the sorting process. You then need to sort through your belongings while taking precautions to protect your health. Remember to be merciless in your decision-making and remind yourself (over and over) that you are not a storage facility for other people's stuff. It's a big job—so let's take those pieces in order...

<u>Make Space for Sorting</u>

If you are like many of my clients, the boxes are usually unmarked (or marked incorrectly) and you have long forgotten what's inside. So it's time to take it box by box. First, clear some space to work. There shouldn't be any items on the floor when you organize, so that is often a good place to start before you begin sorting through boxes.

<u>Toss, Donate or Sell?</u>

Using the techniques we have already discussed, sort through your belongings. Are these items to keep, donate or sell? Try to make these decisions quickly and decisively. As you go through items you haven't seen in years it is easy to stop and take a meandering stroll down memory lane. Our goal is to get through all of this stuff and get it organized and dealt with—so keep reminding yourself to *stay on task*!

Take Precautions

If your attic or basement is dusty or if there are possible contaminants such as insulation or animal dander or waste (mouse scat). Wear a dust mask and gloves and limit your time inside the space. Moving the box outside to look through may be preferable. Wash your hands often to ensure that any spoor or dust doesn't bring on an allergy attack or illness.

I worked with a client who had a rat infestation months before. As we uncovered soiled clothing she made the remark that she would have to wash it in bleach to get it clean. My advice to her was to throw it away, "It isn't worth your health, just toss it out."

Vermin, such as mice or rats, carry any number of diseases. So do birds and small animals. At the very least, they are flea-ridden; at the very worst these creatures (and their droppings) can make you *very* ill. For details on this, go to wikipedia.org and do a search for 'hantavirus.' If you encounter possessions that have animal droppings on them, I suggest that you handle them with gloves and a mask and strongly consider simply throwing the items away instead of trying to clean them.

Be Merciless

Chances are the boxes of clothes you have had stored here for the past five years are out of date, don't fit or just aren't your style any more. The furniture you intended to strip and repair and use 'someday,' is still in the same shape (or worse) than it was back when it was first squirreled away.

We have such grand dreams, plans for furniture we are going to re-finish, sweaters we are going to knit and a thousand "to-do's" for tomorrow. But we run out of time, out of energy, and out of resources. In the end, we can only do so much. So now you must be merciless and move quickly through this myriad of possessions—say no to the outdated clothes two sizes too small, send away the furniture and crafts projects we haven't got time for and give ourselves room to breathe again!

You Are NOT A Storage Facility

Your ex, the former neighbor or a friend that moved half a continent away, asked to store 'just a few things for just a couple of days' in your basement and they are still there three years later. It's time for them to go. Remember the saying "out of sight, out of mind"? Well, their belongings are out of their sight, so they are no longer a burning "Gee, I need to go and get those things" and instead are far more predominantly in your mind. Worse, these possessions that are not yours are sitting in your home and taking up valuable real estate!

Let your friend know that you can no longer store their items for them and set a reasonable deadline for them to come and get their things (or have them shipped). If the deadline comes and goes, get rid of the items. If it isn't important enough for them to come and get them, then they don't want them bad enough. This might be tough for you, no one likes confrontation and it can be difficult—but do you really want to be someone's storage facility? Unless your house is bright orange and has a big PS on the front, you are better off getting it out of there.

Once you have removed the clutter, pull out a broom or vacuum and clear the floors of dirt and dust. Now that you have room to work with, you can consider re-purposing an area once used as storage for other things. You can fit that pool table or the mini-bar or even add a bedroom in your attic. Remember that, although attics and basements are not usually core living areas, with a little bit of work and good planning they can become that 'extra bit of space' that you have been dreaming of for so long.

Garages

Our garages become a dumping ground for so much junk it is mind-boggling. Worse than that, you very quickly run out of room to park your car!

"So what?" you might say, "So I park my car in the driveway, what's the big deal?"

That's a very good question. I have a question in return.

How much did you spend on your car?

If you have 10k, 15k, or even 30k invested in something that is sitting out in the elements, with the rain and hail, wind and snow—you may want to re-think that stance. Even if you spent less money than that, if you don't take care of it and it breaks down, what is your alternative...the bus? If you live here in the Kansas City area, not having a car makes getting around nearly impossible.

However, if you don't have a small shed on your property, you probably use your garage to store lawn equipment and you also probably use it for tools, car 'stuff' and of course, as an overflow for items that can't fit into your kitchen or the rest of your life.

I know that at times, even my own garage is used as a 'staging area' (doesn't that sound much better than storage area) for items that need to be taken away (to be sold, given away, etc.) that we can't have exposed to the elements, but haven't had the opportunity to deal with yet. Broken appliances, empty boxes and, cans and bottles also seem to build up on a regular basis.

Garages are houses for cars and should be used for that primary purpose. That said—most of us still need our garage to serve as *some* kind of storage. So let's talk about possible solutions for getting the clutter off the floor and onto shelves that will work for you.

Let's tackle this mess by first separating into them into categories. Most of us use our garages to store:

- Tools
- Sports equipment
- Auto Maintenance (oil, wiper fluid)
- Lawn & Garden
- General Storage

Let's address each category in order.

Tools

My husband purchased two portable tool boxes to store all of our tools. These quickly became a mess and we would often have to search through both boxes looking for a particular tool—what a time drain! If you have a fair amount of tools, consider purchasing a 'tool tower' with drawers. I have labeled each drawer in a way that makes sense to us and the tools are easy to find and also easy to put back away.

Collect all of your tools and sort them further. At home our categories include:

- Sockets
- Screwdrivers & Nut drivers
- Knives/Scissors/Cutting Implements
- Pliers
- Hammers
- Wrenches/Files/Heavy Stuff
- Saws

When you use an item, put it back as soon as you are done. If you are working on a project that is going to take some time, keep all the applicable tools on location if possible (tools obviously shouldn't be left out where they can be rained on nor have curious toddlers handling them) and then be sure to put them away when the work is complete.

Sports Equipment

"By the time we had finished clearing out the two-car garage, which had been used as storage for over twenty years, we found five bicycles in various states of disrepair. This client had lived alone in her house for nearly thirty years. She dimly recalled getting two of the bicycles, but it had been so long and the garage had been such a mess, she simply didn't remember the others!" – A fellow organizer sharing a recent organizing experience

In my mother's garage there is a pair of white roller skates hanging from a metal rack. I don't think they have been used once since she moved into the house over eighteen years ago. The last time I remember actually seeing her skate in them was when I was a child, over 30 years ago when we lived in Flagstaff, Arizona. They made the trip with her cross-country to the Kansas City area nearly two decades ago and there they have sat ever since.

We keep the mountain bikes and the skis, the tennis rackets and the basketballs. In a corner, the golf clubs gather dust and cobwebs. We feel bad because we aren't using them and we tell ourselves, "This spring I'm going to start biking again." But next spring comes and you find yourself in a walking club or out of town on business or sick with the flu and you forget about the bike. You haven't used the skis since the '80s—the basketballs are flat and cracked—the tennis racket needed to be restrung five years ago.

If you are unwilling to part with these items as you rediscover them, then you must set a 'use by' date. On a piece of notepaper, write down a reasonable date in large clear letters and tape it to the item. Commit to toss, donate or sell those items once the 'use by' date has passed. If you don't have time to get the tennis racket re-strung, then you probably won't be playing tennis anytime soon, either. If the item passes the 'use by' date, get rid of it and reclaim the space!

Auto Maintenance

Cars are usually our second most important investment (after a house if you are a homeowner). Whether you change your own oil and spark plugs or have a mechanic handle it all, it is a good idea to have coolant, windshield wiper fluid and some extra oil on hand at all times. They don't take up an enormous amount of room, but they are essential to good car maintenance.

Try to locate a spot in your garage where these will be out of the way, yet easy to access when needed. Even better, if you have room in the trunk of your car, store the items there—that way you have access to them at all times... no matter where you drive!

Lawn and Garden

If you don't have a storage shed to house your mower and lawn and garden equipment, then try to locate the supplies near a door leading to the yard. For example, in our own house we have a door leading into the main house and also a side door leading to the yard. Next to the side door is a shelving system that holds plant pots, yard chemicals and hand tools. In the winter time, we suspend the mower from the ceiling so that we can park both cars in the garage.

Go through your shovels and other larger lawn tools and make sure that all items are in good shape—no splintered wood handles or broken tips, and weed out any duplicates you may find. I know one client whose garage was such a mess she had purchased four tulip bulb planters over the years—slowly but surely we found them all! She kept one and the other three went to a 'free box' on her front drive and were dispersed among appreciative neighbors.

Hang your tools on the walls of your garage. You can use something as simple as a board with multiple nails to suspend your tools or you can invest in the many different tool hanging organizing solutions offered at home improvement stores—whichever you prefer.

<u>General Storage</u>

General storage includes everything from boxes of personal belongings to extra household supplies (paper towels) and even paint.

- Personal belongings—Label it, label it, LABEL IT! You aren't going to know what is in a box a year from now unless you label it. Be as clear as possible and make sure you place the labels on one end and on one side, for good measure.
- Household supplies—Garages can be perfect for storing those extra paper plates and paper towels. I also keep my cleaning caddy (one caddy for the entire house) in the garage. I suggest locating these items close to the entrance to the house for easier access. You don't want to have to traipse through the entire length of the garage to get that bag of plastic silverware when you are busy getting dinner ready for your guests. In our garage, household items and cleaning supplies are located right next to the door to the house.
- Paint—Keep paint clearly labeled. I usually slap on a big label (2"x4") and write with a permanent marker the room I used the paint in and the year. I also try to dab a little bit of paint right on the label as an example. Remember, paint is flammable, so keep it away from heat sources!

Advanced Organization

Organizing Your Finances

Still hanging on to that checkbook register and balancing it by hand? Is that really the best use of your time?

Years ago, I was married to a man who seemed to regard a woman being interested in household finance as an oddity. He was rather amused by my wish to be a part of the financial decision-making. He was used to paying all of the bills, keeping track of all the accounts and really didn't see a reason why I should be involved in any way.

I persisted—I wanted to find out just where all the money was going. His attitude changed from amused to annoyed and what followed was an hour-long, bill-paying marathon. This was all done by hand, with notations made on each credit card statement as to the check # and amount, envelopes to lick and stamp, and then of course, we had to balance the checkbook. I was so turned off by the experience (mainly his attitude), that I let him handle it all, until the day I found myself in the middle of a nasty divorce. And let me tell you, not knowing where all of the money was going was not good for either of us. I found out, too late, that my soon to be ex-husband had been overspending. Our spending exceeded our income by approximately $500 per month and this had been going on for over three years!

I began using Quicken and I have never looked back. Balance a checkbook by hand? Have to write on each bill how much I paid and when and with what check number? Hah! What took us over an hour that one day nearly two decades ago, I can get done in ten minutes with Quicken. I can also run reports in seconds—something that would probably take hours, if I had to look it up manually.

I just decided to test the latter claim by running a quick report. I went to Quicken and clicked on Spending, asked Quicken to show me my total spending for groceries and dining out last month. The answer? $1,068.78. That's right in line with what I expected – I have my budget set at $1,000 for a family of four for food and dining out each month.

Now even if you don't think that is something you will need, consider this next scenario:

A few months ago, I receive a letter from a collections company claiming I hadn't paid a medical bill. Since I'm rather [ahem] *organized,* I was skeptical. I looked for the doctor's name on the bill and then ran a quick report in Quicken. Sure enough, it showed up not only as payment sent, but reconciled (since I reconcile my bank statement from the bank with Quicken each month). I made a call to the doctor's office and, after just a few minutes of searching, they realized they had applied my payment to the wrong account. They called the collection agency and withdrew the collections request immediately.

Now if you had kept all of your records and everything was in the right order, than you wouldn't have any problem finding this mistake and getting it fixed just like I did. The difference is, it took me two minutes to find that record of payment... how long will it take you?

How much is your time worth? Would you rather sit down in front of a computer for a few minutes, process and schedule all of your payments, then go off to enjoy a fine spring day—or do you want to spend the next hour and a half paying bills?

<u>Creating (and following) a Budget</u>

I will be discussing how to create a budget in Excel (or equivalent spreadsheet program) in the next section. Hang in there, this is a whole new section updated for 2018!

<u>Recommended Software</u>

It isn't enough to have a budget. You really need to know WHERE your money is going so that you can change your behaviors or cut other expenses in order to not overextend yourself.

Over the past 15+ years, I have used a number of software programs to help me track my expenses.

I personally recommend Quicken now that Microsoft is no longer producing Microsoft Money. There are several version of Quicken, because I also run a small business, I prefer the Home and Business version – it is relatively easy to work with.

You may also want to look into free, open-source accounting software. You will find those listed under Open-Source Software in Section 4—Resources.

I track everything from debts (credit cards, house loan and student loan) to our different accounts (checking, savings, 401k and money market) all in Quicken.

With financial software, you have instant updates on your balance with far less margin of error (error on data entry side only) than a handwritten check register. Keep this in mind—you double your chance for error using the handwritten method—you can write down the wrong amount or you can make an error in calculation. With accounting software, the only errors come from the data entry side of things; the software does all of the calculations, which cuts in half your margin of error!

Another wonderful feature is the ability to create budgets, plans for debt reduction and run reports to find out exactly where you are spending your money. If you are sure you paid for that magazine subscription but the company is claiming you didn't, do a 'Search by Payee' and find it in seconds instead of searching through your handwritten check registers for a copy.

Receipts

I recommend that you only keep your receipts for 'big ticket' items in a folder/envelope. 'Big ticket' items are appliance or electronic purchases usually. Keep these indefinitely and pair them with any warranty information you might have for the item in case you need to return it due to malfunction.

The rest of your personal receipts (for gas, regular day-to-day purchases, etc.) can be kept in a revolving folder by month, if you think you may need them again. I personally do not return many items, so once I have processed the accounting of the payment in Quicken, I usually dispose of the receipt.

However, for those who do return items on a regular basis, keep in mind that most department stores now have a fixed date for returns (usually 30-90 days from date of purchase). In your case I recommend that you add a set of receipt folders labeled by month (January, February, March, etc.) and then purge anything older than three months.

If any receipt is for either work or business expenses—<u>absolutely</u> keep it! For my business receipts, I have twelve folders, clearly labeled by month. This provides me with ease of reference—if I need to check a receipt, I simply look in that particular month's folder. I also have a Year folder. At the end of the year I combine all of the business receipts for the previous months into the year folder and write the total amount on the outside of the folder. This folder then goes into my tax folder so that I can reference it when I file my taxes.

Online Banking

Many banks offer online banking and even online bill pay to their customers. Free of charge. Commerce Bank is a good example, although there are many others. Check with your bank and see if they offer either of these services.

This is extremely handy if you are traveling and need to check on your bank balance. You simply log in to the bank website through a secure connection and enter your username and unique password (sometimes there are additional safety measures in place if you are not logging in from your usual computer). The best part of online banking is the ability to pay bills. The bank will mail the payment directly to the biller—you save on the cost of stamps—as well as time. I save over $105 in postage each year by using online banking. You can transfer funds, pay bills and check account balances all with the click of a button! How easy is that?!

<u>Direct Draft</u>

Similar to online banking is direct draft. A direct draft is where a company (such as a utility or mortgage company) withdraws payments from your bank account directly, instead of you authorizing the payment directly through your bank account. *I strongly advise against this.* Even if you have a bill that never changes, never goes up or down, having a direct draft means a loss of control that can potentially cause huge problems.

A few years back I re-financed my mortgage. I re-financed with the same mortgage company (Chase) and at the time the old mortgage payment was set up as a direct draft from my checking account. The re-finance went through in November and we were not supposed to have a payment due until January. I checked online and the information on the old mortgage had disappeared from the Chase website. I assumed this meant that they knew the old mortgage had been paid off and that in January the new mortgage would begin.

One week later, multiple checks began to bounce. The mortgage company had taken a direct draft of the old mortgage! After a couple of panicked phone calls to Chase and also to my bank explaining the situation, we were able to have the payment reversed FIVE days later. Over $200 in bounced check fees had been assessed and the representative at Chase assured me that it was entirely my fault and that they were not responsible for the charges! Thankfully, our bank was very understanding. Due to our excellent credit and banking history they rescinded all of the overdraft charges.

Every few months, I get a very nice letter from Chase asking us why we don't use direct draft and assuring us that it is so *easy* and *convenient.* I promptly shred the letter and remember the representative who assured me that not only was it entirely my fault they didn't know to stop drafting our account, but that he "had no boss" and that, no, I would not be allowed to speak to anyone else regarding the fiasco.

Instead of direct draft, I pay our mortgage through online bill-pay with my bank as a recurring monthly payment. It took me one minute to set up, four years ago, and it pays the bill each month and will until I issue the command to stop paying it. Direct draft takes bill-paying out of your control and you run the risk of a company accepting absolutely no accountability for their actions.

Keeping clear financial records saves you time and money. By automating your bill-paying and using accounting software you streamline and simplify what was once an onerous weekly task. You also reduce the chance for error, while keeping your finances under your control through utilizing online bill-payment systems.

Good financial organization is very important—and so is incorporating sound time management techniques, which we will now discuss.

Time Management

"Life is what happens to you while you're busy making other plans." – John Lennon

These days, time truly does seem to fly by. Hours become days, days into weeks and weeks into months. It felt as though I turned around twice and my newborn infant was now a toddler.

Years ago, while writing the first edition of this book, I was discussing it with my daughter's pediatrician. "How wonderful! Will you include a section on time management?" she asked. When I told her yes, she said, "All I ever hear, from parents who stay at home with their kids to the CEO's of corporations, is 'I never have enough time.' Write about that, because everyone needs help organizing their time and figuring out how to be more effective each day."

Thank you, Dr. Glotzbach, I will do just that!

Part of being organized means knowing *where* you are going and *when* you need to be there. It also helps to define your objectives by setting daily goals, achieving tasks and displaying action and accomplishment in all facets of your life. This can cover a whole range of areas:

- Physical maintenance, such as:
    - Have your teeth cleaned and checked every six months
    - Schedule a physical for once a year and schedule a mammogram/prostate exam as recommended by your physician for your health and age bracket
    - Join an aerobics/yoga/walking program
    - Schedule regular haircuts/manicures

- Work/Career, such as:
    - Learn a new program or facet of your job to enhance your chances of promotion
    - Take a class/earn a degree
    - Read a book/learn a new skill
- Friends/Family, such as:
    - Regular medical checkups for kids
    - Activities with friends
    - Planning for upcoming birthdays and anniversaries
- Household, such as:
    - Scheduling regular oil changes and maintenance for your car
    - Changing the air filter in your furnace (every 6-8 weeks!)
    - Fixing the dripping faucet
    - Setting a reminder to plant fall bulbs or prepare your lawn for winter

These are just a few examples of areas of time management. You can use a day planner or time management software on your computer to help you get started. Whichever works best for you, handwritten or digital, start using it and you will find that you can add at least another hour of productivity to your day (dare I say 25th Hour?!) by focusing your priorities and defining your goals.

There are entire books devoted to this subject, but we simply don't have the room to go into great detail on the subject. Instead, I will simply introduce you to some basic tools of time management and encourage you to explore more of this area on your own.

Agenda/Day Planner

As you will read below, I prefer to have my time management in digital form. However, if you do not have a computer, an agenda or day planner is an excellent tool for keeping track of your upcoming appointments and 'to-do's.' In the past (before Microsoft Outlook or Google Calendar) I used Franklin-Covey day planners. This particular day planner is very well laid out. It includes goal-defining sections and also task lists.

Note: take the time to read any directions or suggested tips that are included with the day planner. It will help you to use the day planner more effectively.

Google Calendar

A decade ago I was a tried and true Microsoft Outlook kind of gal. These days, while I still use Outlook to check email, Google Calendar has replaced Outlook as my go to destination.

I am busy. I run a small business, write, am the primary caretaker for my dad who has dementia, we are renovating three properties to be future rentals or Airbnb units, and I have neighborhood obligations as well. Being able to add my entire schedule (and my husband's, my dad's and my daughter's) keeps me on track!

I use it to organize all of my appointments – color-coding the appointments for each member of my family – and also for tracking local events, weekend "to do's" and other reminders.

I'm going to show you some shots of my calendar on Google and point out some of the benefits of switching from a hand-written day planner, Outlook, or nothing at all, to working with Google Calendar.

I work exclusively with it set on the month view. What can I say? I like to plan ahead and be able to see an entire month at a time!

Calendar:

Google Calendar is very handy for scheduling appointments. I use it to track upcoming events and business appointments for both my housecleaning and organizing businesses. You can even create multiple calendars to track different members of your household. I especially like the ability to color-code activities and I have edited the colors to mean different things, such as:

Aqua = Birthdays

Yellow = Cleaning biz appointments

Light Green = A class I am teaching

Dark Green = Marketing schedule

Lavender = My youngest child's schedule

Light blue = Appointments for my dad

Dark Blue = My husband's schedule

You can also schedule recurring appointments automatically. For example, if you go to yoga class every Tuesday, create the event and click on the "Edit event" box. That will open a box that looks like this:

You can even specify how many recurrences. It takes far less time than writing appointments down by hand in an agenda.

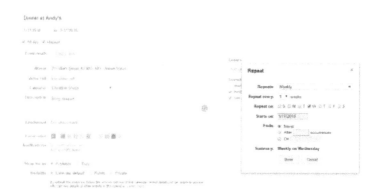

You can also specify how you wish to view the calendar (Day, Week or Month). Here it is in Week view...

And in Day view...

Oops, it looks like I need to contact that client and reschedule her cleaning to another day. Her normal cleaning day is every four weeks on a Monday, but I imagine she won't want me showing up at 9 a.m. on New Year's Day!

Contacts:

The Contacts section is your Address book in digital form. There are many different views, I prefer the 'detailed address card' view because when I view my entire Contacts list, I can also see any applicable account numbers or notes I have added for a particular contact.

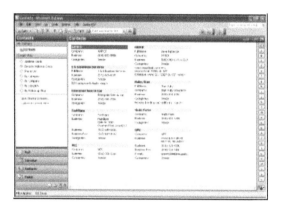

As you can see, I do still use Outlook for my Contacts. I keep them in both Google Gmail AND Outlook, but I prefer Outlook's display format.

Tasks:

The Tasks section of Outlook is your 'to-do' list in digital form. You can schedule tasks years in the future. When my husband and I installed a tile floor in January 2007, the directions on the grout sealer advised re-sealing the grout every three years. So I entered a task in Outlook to remind me on January 1st, 2010 to 're-seal the kitchen floor.'

I use the Tasks section of Outlook to schedule all kinds of reminders for business and personal tasks.

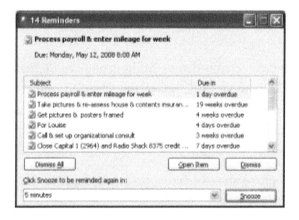

As you can see, several tasks are overdue, but they are still there and continue to remind me to get to them. Each week, I look over my task list and address as many as I can. You can also set recurring reminders in Outlook. For example, I have a recurring reminder set to change our furnace filter every eight weeks. When I complete the task, I right-click and choose 'Mark Complete.' It then reminds me eight weeks later, to change the furnace filter again.

Having Outlook (or some other personal time management software) saves you a great deal of time by making it so easy to move appointments ahead, mark items complete and have lists right at your fingertips.

Organizing Digital Photos

"What kind of pictures are you taking? Break them down into categories—for example, if you take pictures of weddings, label them by the last name and the date. Some of my folders include categories such as: people pictures, pets, weather and interior decorating. I even have a folder labeled 'weeds'!" —My response to a class attendee who had over 10,000 digital photos to organize

Oh, the wonders of the digital age we live in! For mere pennies, we can now take photo after photo, upload them to our computers and erase 'red eye,' crop, zoom and resize. We can pick and choose our favorites and then transmit the files electronically to be printed on our home photo printers or online and pick them up at a local photo shop.

Within the space of a few years, digital cameras have become affordable and so very easy to use. Shortly after my second daughter was born—a full eighteen years after her older sister, I asked my husband for a better digital camera. I received an Olympus 8.0 mega pixel with SLR body, wonder machine, as an early birthday gift. I had already been taking a large number of photos of our infant daughter; this just encouraged me to take even more!

But what to do with all of those photos—how could I put them in some semblance of order, so that I could find them again?

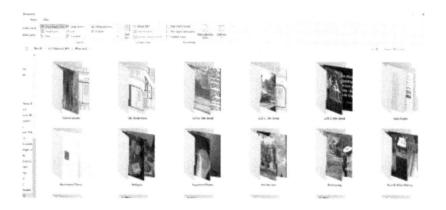

Here is my main Picture folder. I organized my pictures first by category. I like to get a glimpse of what I'm looking at, so I chose 'View' and 'Thumbnails.' Some examples of categories we use for our own pictures are:

- Events
- Wildlife
- Scenery
- 10th Street Garden

Under many of the main categories are sub-folders. For example, I have created separate folders by Year under the 10th Street Garden category (2014, 22015, etc.).

In my Cottage West folder shown above, a property we are renovating to use as an Airbnb, I have labeled folders with the year first, the month, and then a brief description of what it is.

For example: 2014 – 08 – Clean out and yard work

I will be adding many of the pictures to a book I am working on, *I Bought a House for $25-The Journey from Derelict to Beauty* and I want to show the progression from the neglected house we purchased in

July 2014 to the cute bungalow that will eventually house visitors and tourists to our fair city.

Having my photographs clearly organized helps with that process.

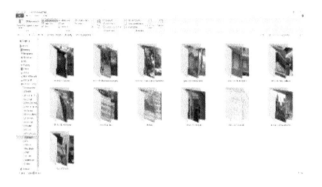

In the next image, I list the subject (my daughter Emily), the Year and the Month. *Note: be sure to use '01' instead of '1' or 'January', this helps keep them in numerical order for ease of reference later.*

Keeping your pictures organized according to category and date, makes finding them later a 'snap.' I often get requests from friends or family to pull up celebrations or events from years past. I can easily find them and then send them off in an email or order prints online.

Whether you are organizing your photographs, your closets or your garage the premise remains the same—being organized means you will have more time for the important things in life—whether that is curling up with a good novel or cuddling with that special someone.

In this section, we have discussed core living areas, other living areas, advanced organizational techniques, and we have gone room-by-room. If you haven't done any organizing—get started right now. Take it room by room, visualize what each room could become and make it happen!

Then read on, because next we are going to discuss techniques on staying organized—now, and for years to come.

Organized Finances and Budgeting

I'm going to step out on a limb here and suggest you take a big step and create (and stick) to a budget. You might have come to this book looking for advice on actual physical clutter, but being organized also means knowing exactly where you are spending your money and how you can go about altering those spending habits so that you:

- Live within your means
- Reduce or eliminate debt
- Increase your income
- Plan for retirement

And I have a confession to make as well. In the decade between the first and second edition of this book, my husband and I found ourselves in full Chapter 7 bankruptcy in late 2010.

We were upside down in our mortgage, impossibly behind in credit card debt, and we were not living within our means or planning for retirement.

Recovering from bankruptcy was not easy. We changed our spending habits and have tried to avoid new debt wherever possible.

As a result, just seven years after bankruptcy we now own four houses: our original home in Belton which we now rent out, our home we live in Kansas City, and two small homes we are in the process of renovating so that we can either rent them out or use them as Airbnb properties.

Each month, we use one credit card for nearly all of our spending. It gives us cash rewards of 1-2% depending on the transaction and we use it for everything from groceries to gas, utility bills, insurance payments, and the daily needs of our household. And each month, without fail, we pay off the entire balance, making sure we do not incur any interest penalties.

We can do this because we have sat down and figured out exactly where our money is going and (in a pinch) what we can cut to afford something extra.

I've provided a simplified version of the Excel spreadsheet I use to plot out and adjust for our monthly living expenses.

And here are a couple of points to share...

You will see two columns, Monthly and Annual. Any payment or expense that is not a normal average monthly cost goes in the Annual column. I also refer to them as Non-Monthly Expenses.

So here is the first tip I have for you:

Tip #1 - Have two separate checking accounts, preferably at the same bank – your main checking and your non-monthly expense checking.

When you fill out your own Excel spreadsheet (go to http://bit.ly/2zNN89B to download your own copy) you will put amounts in either the Monthly or Annual columns.

"But wait! Some of my payments are twice a year, others, like car repairs fall into the 'whenever they are needed' category!"

Yes, that's why we just put all of those into the Annual expense column. For example, you might see that I have Car Maintenance and Repair pegged as $3,000 in this spreadsheet. We typically learn about fixes we need to make at least twice per year – at our regular oil changes. And now that we have aging vehicles, I have pegged our annual expenses for maintenance at closer to $5,000.

Here is the nice part about divvying up your expenses into Monthly and Non-Monthly categories: less bumps and dips in your monthly income.

Expenses:	Monthly	Annual
Automobile/Commute Expense		
Car Insurance (avg)	*NME*	*$ 800.00*
Car Maintenance & Repair	*NME*	*$ 3,000.00*
Car Payment	$ 250.00	
Fuel	$ 200.00	
Children		
Allowance	$ 25.00	
Education	NME	*$ 200.00*
Summer Camp		*$ 500.00*
Savings	$ 100.00	
Food, Dining, Alcohol		
Alcohol	$ 75.00	
Dining Out	$ 300.00	
Groceries	$ 700.00	
Household Expenses		
Clothing and Shoes		*$ 1,000.00*
Entertainment	$ 20.00	
General Expenses	$ 150.00	
Gifts Given/Birthdays/Christmas	*NME*	*$ 1,000.00*
Mortgage/Rent	$ 800.00	
Pets	$ 75.00	
Travel/Vacation		*$ 2,000.00*
Health Expenses		
Co-Pays	$ 60.00	
Medical Insurance	$ 80.00	
Prescriptions	$ 50.00	
Utilities		
Alarm System		*$ 200.00*
Cable/Netflix/etc	$ 50.00	
Cell phones	$ 100.00	
Electric	$ 200.00	
Gas (utility)	$ 90.00	
Internet	$ 50.00	
Trash Service	$ 15.00	
Water	$ 50.00	
Credit Debt		
Credit Card/Loan 1	$ 150.00	$ -
Credit Card/Loan 2	$ 300.00	
Credit Card/Loan 3	$ 400.00	
Taxes		
Property Taxes (Auto)	*NME*	*$ 500.00*
Property Taxes (Real Estate)		*$ 2,000.00*
Property Taxes (Other)	*NME*	*$ -*
Property Repair, Maintenance and Improvements		
Property Repair/Improvements	$ 400.00	
Lawn and Garden		
Savings and Investments		
Savings - General Emergency Fund	$ 200.00	
Savings - Long Term	$ 300.00	
Investments/401k	$ 300.00	
Non-Monthly Expenses		*$ 11,200.00*
NME Account (set aside and draw from as needed)	*$ 933.33*	
Total Expenses:	**$ 6,423.33**	

Income:		
Income #1	$ 3,000.00	
Income #2	$ 3,856.67	
Total Income:	$ 6,856.67	
Overage/Shortfall:	$433.33	

Expenses:	Monthly	Annual
Automobile/Commute Expense		
Car Insurance (avg)	NME	$ 800.00
Car Maintenance & Repair	NME	$ 3,000.00
Car Payment	$ 250.00	
Fuel	$ 200.00	
Children		
Allowance	$ 25.00	
Education	NME	$ 200.00
Summer Camp		$ 500.00
Savings	$ 100.00	
Food, Dining, Alcohol		
Alcohol	$ 75.00	
Dining Out	$ 300.00	
Groceries	$ 700.00	
Household Expenses		
Clothing and Shoes		$ 1,000.00
Entertainment	$ 20.00	
General Expenses	$ 150.00	
Gifts Given/Birthdays/Christmas	NME	$ 1,000.00
Mortgage/Rent	$ 800.00	
Pets	$ 75.00	
Travel/Vacation		$ 2,000.00
Health Expenses		
Co-Pays	$ 60.00	
Medical Insurance	$ 80.00	
Prescriptions	$ 50.00	

After you enter all of your data – you will see a total of non-monthly expenses in the grayed in area. This is your estimated total for the year. Now, we can't plan for everything, but the more you are able to set aside, the easier those bumps in the road will be. In the sample budget, you can see that the total is $11,200. Divide that by 12, and you will see $933.33 is now in the monthly column. That is the amount you will deposit into your Non-Monthly Expense account each month.

Then it is a simple matter of transferring the money back into your main checking account to pay for any expenses. OR you could simply issue payment out of the NME account directly to the creditor for your car expense, or other non-monthly expenditures.

Utilities		
Alarm System		$ 200.00
Cable/Netflix/etc	$ 50.00	
Cell phones	$ 100.00	
Electric	$ 200.00	
Gas (utility)	$ 90.00	
Internet	$ 50.00	
Trash Service	$ 15.00	
Water	$ 50.00	
Credit Debt		
Credit Card/Loan 1	$ 150.00	$ -
Credit Card/Loan 2	$ 300.00	
Credit Card/Loan 3	$ 400.00	
Taxes		
Property Taxes (Auto)	NME	$ 500.00
Property Taxes (Real Estate)		$ 2,000.00
Property Taxes (Other)	NME	$ -
Property Repair, Maintenance and Improvements		
Property Repair/Improvements	$ 400.00	
Lawn and Garden		
Savings and Investments		
Savings - General Emergency Fund	$ 200.00	
Savings - Long Term	$ 300.00	
Investments/401k	$ 300.00	
Non-Monthly Expenses		$ 11,200.00
NME Account (set aside and draw from as needed)	$ 933.33	
Total Expenses:	$ 6,423.33	

Knowing where you spend your money each month is answered by having financial software (Quicken) and tracking it through categories, and having a budget is the step *after* you have a handle on what your spending habits are.

Having the Non-Monthly Expense account eases the financial bumps from your month-to-month living expenses.

Income:		
Income #1	$ 3,000.00	
Income #2	$ 3,856.67	
Total Income:	$ 6,856.67	
Overage/Shortfall:	$433.33	

There is one other suggestion I have when it comes to budgets – add in some room for error. Even with the NME account helping to maintain your financial equilibrium from month to month – life can get hairy. We simply cannot plan for every contingency, so I advise you make sure that the overage/shortfall box have at least $200 in the black as part of your budget, preferably $300. I call it my "slush" – but let me tell you, no matter how much I plan out our finances, having that 'slush' has made all the difference in the world when we have had unexpected expenses.

I have found that creating a budget (and sticking to it) has been invaluable to getting my family out of debt and on the right track for retirement. Knowing *where* you are spending your money allows you to evaluate whether you want to reduce spending in one area and possibly increase it (or save it) in another.

Having Quicken and online banking has allowed me to easily schedule payments in order to never have late payments on anything, which has also led to a better credit score with the big three (Transunion, Equifax and Experian) over time.

Section 3: Staying Organized

| Page

Lifestyle Changes

"Promise me you'll always remember: You're braver than you believe, and stronger than you seem, and smarter than you think." —Christopher Robin to Pooh

Over and over again I hear my clients ask, "But how do I get my house to *stay* this way?" I used to wonder if they were hoping for some magic answer. Organizing came so naturally to me that it seemed silly that they would ask—but when you are in the thick of it, you often can't see the simple facts of the problem:

Fact One—It took time for it to get this bad.

Fact Two—It takes time and hard work to get rid of the clutter.

Fact Three—The clutter will come back if you don't make some basic lifestyle changes.

These lifestyle changes are not necessarily difficult, but they do take repetition and commitment. You have worked hard to get your space organized, so reward that hard work by keeping the clutter from returning!

It's easy for me to breeze in and show clients how to organize, but unless I give them the tools to stay organized, I'll see them again, all too soon. I don't believe that it is ethical for me to take someone's money and just keep coming back again and again, without affecting some kind of permanent change. Sometimes circumstances dictate that a client calls me in again, but hopefully it is for a different part of their house!

So how do you get to the point where you don't need a professional organizer or marathon organizing sessions any more? I believe that it starts by first examining how you spend your days and what kind of shopping decisions you make. Then you can begin to incorporate into your day-to-day life some effective organizational strategies for limiting clutter before it begins—thereby creating better habits and a more organized state of living.

By employing a few lifestyle changes, you will stay organized in the days and weeks that follow your initial organizing efforts. Remember, it isn't enough to simply clear out the clutter, you must also learn new habits to prevent the clutter from re-occurring. You can do that through a variety of methods, and I will discuss each in detail below.

So let's get started!

But first, if you haven't given yourself a pat on the back, now is the time. By now you have begun to clear up at least some of your clutter and you are well on your way to a better, less stressful life. Congratulations!

Your Daily Activities

Everyone's life is different and so are their daily routines. I'll make some assumptions here and talk about a fictitious person we will call Angela:

Every morning Angela wakes up, rolls out of bed and makes her way to the kitchen. Twice, in the last week, she has stubbed her toe on her son's scooter, which is leaning against a wall in the narrow hallway. Angela limps toward the kitchen and searches for a clean cup while the coffee is brewing. Not able to find a clean coffee cup (the sink is full and the dishwasher is only half-filled with dirty dishes), she settles for a quick swish of water in a relatively clean looking cup and sits down at her table, shoving her son's books aside so she can fit her coffee cup on a level surface.

Half an hour later she finishes her coffee and heads for the shower, leaving her cup on the table with just a smidgen of coffee in it. She pulls off her pajamas as the shower water heats and tosses them into a heap near the bathroom sink. But before she can get into the shower she has to find her towel, which is still on the bed, crumpled and still slightly damp from yesterday morning's shower.

With just a couple lifestyle changes, Angela's morning (and her son's) could be very different. There is a literal parade of 'ifs' here:

- If Angela established a five-minute evening routine of picking up toys and belongings before bed, she wouldn't have stubbed her toe or had to fight for a corner of the kitchen table space.
- If she had spent just three minutes loading the dishwasher while her coffee brewed, she wouldn't have a mess of dirty dishes to come home to in the evening.
- If Angela had put her not quite empty coffee cup in the sink or dishwasher, it wouldn't have spilled coffee dregs on her son's homework as he rushed to meet the school bus later that morning.

- If she had put away her towel after she showered the day before she wouldn't have a damp and smelly towel to dry herself with.

Now let's consider Beth's morning:

Beth rolls out of bed, grabs the empty plate and glass next to her bed (a late-night snack before bed) and heads for the kitchen. Her preschool-aged son still has trouble with the idea of putting things away the evening before, but the ten minutes were well spent last night—his Duplo blocks are all put away and her path to the kitchen is clear.

She rinses the plate and glass and puts them in the dishwasher while her coffee brews. Coffee cup in hand, she sits down at the kitchen table with a magazine and reads for fifteen minutes, while sipping her coffee. She also starts a list of priorities for the day, writing them down on a slip of paper. When she has finished with the coffee, she rinses out the cup and puts it in the dishwasher, then starts the cleaning cycle. She also makes a quick pass with the dishcloth and wipes up the coffee drips.

Beth then heads for the shower—takes aim from the bathroom and scores two points—her pajamas land in the clothes basket with a single toss. She also picks up two items on the sink and puts them away in their proper homes, while she waits for her shower water to heat.

So how much time has Beth invested in making her life a little more clutter-free? Fifteen minutes at most and that's counting the toy pick-up time the evening before. And what is her reward for fifteen minutes of work? A clean kitchen table, no stubbed toes, clean dishes, a fresh towel and a laundry basket that is ready to pick up and take to the washer. She is also teaching her son skills he will need later in life—ones that will help keep him organized and responsible in the long school years to come.

So think for a moment about your life and your daily routines.

- What do you do when you first wake up?
- How can you combine tasks?

- How can you streamline activities to include little clutter-reducing tasks along the way?

The simple act of walking from one end of your house to another can be altered to include clutter-reducing strategies. As you move about your day, through your house, into your car and away to work—incorporate simple lifestyle changes. You will find these opportunities surround us:

- clean out a purse while you wait for your carpool partner to arrive
- tidy your kitchen while you wait for a meal to heat in the microwave
- make your bed when you first get up and are standing right there
- incorporate tidying your bathroom or dusting your furniture as you pass through a room

The opportunities are endless!

Shopping—Purpose or Passion?

When you go shopping, is it with a particular purpose in mind? Or are you just in the mood to spend some money and blow off some steam?

Many of my clients confess that they shop when they are upset or depressed or stressed out. I can relate to that—the last time my husband and I had a fight I bought over $100 worth of books!

I am not a therapist, and I don't play one on TV, but I think that we do have a spending problem, individually, and as a nation. I think that at some level, we are seeking to fill the holes in our lives with things instead of people, belongings instead of relationships. If this sounds at all familiar, then perhaps it might be worth your time to examine your shopping behaviors more closely.

I pose the following questions to many of my clients:

- Do you find yourself shopping when you don't really need anything?
- Do you feel compelled to buy something, whether you need it or not, 'just because'?
- Do you have bags of purchases that you've brought into the house and then just never put away or used and eventually forgot you even bought?
- Do you look at purchases and wonder why in the world you bought that item?
- Have you ever discovered that you just purchased an item identical to one you already owned by accident?

It seems to be a cultural expectation that women are shopping junkies, always out for our next fix in the shoe department. It doesn't have to be that way and it causes far more stress and anxiety down the road when you finally have to thin out the clutter. Inevitably, you will be recompensed with pennies on the dollar for your time and investment—plus you've stored it for an untold length of time in your home, allowing an item to live rent-free and bring in no profit or benefit of any kind!

Bottom line? Don't shop when you are stressed or depressed or angry. Here are some other tips to keep in mind before you swipe that debit card:

- Set yourself a monthly budget for spending in a particular category and stick to it (financial software makes tracking this very easy!)
- If you see something you just 'have to have,' wait for a week and then return and buy it if you still feel the same way.
- Instead of shopping, go for a walk or see a movie or travel to an area you haven't been to before.
- If you are a compulsive book collector like me, I suggest a visit to the library—imagine all of those thousands of books, free for you to look at!

By all means, window shop away, but keep a tighter hold on your pocketbook and start brainstorming better ways to spend your time. The world is big and it is full of adventures that outstrip even the best bargain-hunting you have ever indulged in. Whereas compulsive shopping and out-of-control spending depletes our bank accounts and fills our lives with more and more clutter. Break the cycle and you will enrich your life.

Economy of Movement—Part II

Remember my explanation of Economy of Movement earlier in the book? Well, here it is again, an excellent tool for clutter control.

As I explained in Part I, Economy of Movement means incorporating organizing while conserving your energy at the same time.

When you walk in the door from work, take a brief moment to hang up your coat and purse and put your keys and cell phone in a bowl. This is a far better option than having to put them away later (an extra trip to the coat closet).

When you get up in the morning, pick up that dirty glass next to your bed and take it with you into the kitchen as you head there to make coffee.

Stage items to go to other parts of the house by placing them next to the door out of that particular room and just bend down and pick them up as you move from one room to another.

Incorporate these simple movements into your daily routine and watch your life *stay* organized. It will quickly become second nature!

Re-visiting Premises

During the organizing process there may have been quite a few things you kept. Some of them may have been items that you really didn't need, but you weren't ready to let go of. That's okay, it happens to a lot of us. What happens next is what I like to call re-visiting premises. First—let some time go by, maybe three to six months, and then re-visit areas of your house where you had difficulty letting go of the items. These areas may still be still on the edge of clutter. Perhaps you have a drawer or shelf that defied your best efforts or you have several boxes of heirlooms and family possessions you just couldn't bear to go through. Take the time to look them over again and ask yourself:

- Why am I keeping this item?
- Is this item being used?
- Will it ever be used?
- Is it taking up valuable space that could be occupied by more important things?
- Could someone else use it right now?

Make Regular Donations

I hope I have already convinced you that donating clothing, furniture and other items is a worthwhile endeavor. There are so many people out there who live on the edge of poverty. Years ago, I was one of them and was more than happy to be able to find and buy used items at a heavily discounted price.

Without stores like Goodwill, the Salvation Army and Savers—both my daughter and I would have been wearing thread-bare, out-grown clothes. Instead, we were able to dress simply but tastefully and even feel a little fashionable!

Donating is a win-win on all sides:

- You get a tax write-off and less clutter
- The charity you donate to profits by selling the items at a deeply discounted price
- The individual buying the item is able to purchase something they would not otherwise be able to afford

So please, donate, donate, DONATE!

Limit Your Future Purchases

Earlier, I spoke about examining why you shop and possible alternatives to spending. Limiting your purchases is more than just NOT shopping, it is learning to be clear and reasonable about what you need *right now*.

In my pantry are five jars of pimientos. I use pimientos perhaps once a year when I make an old family recipe we call Hoferkampf. Other than that one time in a year, I have no need for pimientos. I am not sure how I ended up with five jars, but that is what I have. My husband pointed to them the other day and said, "Please, for the love of all that is good and holy, don't buy any more of those *things*!" Five jars of pimientos is simply four jars too many. We had a good laugh over them and I tossed out three of the older jars.

Limit your purchases when grocery shopping by:

- When you are shopping, make a list before you leave. Look through the flyers for your local grocery store (ours are delivered to our door weekly) and write down any specials you think you need. Double-check your pantry and/or refrigerator to make sure you don't already have the item in question.
- Make up a menu for the rest of the week of meal plans then only purchase the food products you will need for your menu.
- Avoid impulse purchases or at least limit them to one per visit. If you are faced with three items that aren't on your list but seem like 'such a great deal,' pick one and put the other two back where you found them.

Consider Hiring a Service

Having your house cleaned or your lawn mowed can be absolutely fantastic. There's nothing quite like coming home after a long day and seeing a well maintained lawn or noticing how everything sparkles inside your home—no dust bunnies or crumbs on the counters.

Before I started 25th Hour Organizing, I ran a housecleaning business. Time after time, I heard the same thing from my female clients, "Having my house cleaned is something I do for *me*. It's like going to the spa!"

Obviously, financial considerations take precedence here, but if you can afford to have either a lawn service or a cleaning service you may find that it is money well spent. You can use that extra time to organize a closet, learn a new computer program or spend time with a friend or family member.

Less IS More

Do you find yourself overwhelmed with gifts, hand-me-downs or "I saw this and thought of you," from friends and family? It is a fine line we tread when dealing with people we care about. We don't want to be rude and yet we don't want to be overrun with stuff.

So what do we do?

Encourage your loved ones to give you gifts that don't add to your clutter, such as:

- take you out to dinner at your favorite restaurant
- send you a gift card to your favorite store
- make a donation in your name to a charity of your choice

Commit to Regular Check-Ups

Life gets messy. No matter how organized you learn to be, you will still have to go back and briefly re-organize some areas. Consider committing to regular organizing sprees, so that things never get this bad again.

Break down the areas of your home into seasons. If you commit to regularly revisiting these areas each year, your house will stay clutter-free for years to come!

Recommended Scheduled 'Spruce-Ups'

Spring—garages, basements, attics

Summer—kitchens and bathrooms

Fall—kids and school

Winter—closets, nooks and crannies

| Page

Maintaining—Room by Room

In Section 2, I went room-by-room through your core living areas. Here are some good tips on staying organized in the most heavily used rooms of your home.

Kitchens

While You Are Waiting

While you are waiting for your coffee to brew or you bread to finish toasting:

- Wipe down counters
- Empty or reload the dishwasher
- Move any empty bottles or cans to the recycle container
- Tidy the kitchen table
- Alphabetize your spices

Use a shopping list

I try to limit my shopping to once per week, which usually falls somewhere around the weekend. Before I go shopping, I sit down at the kitchen table to make two lists – one is the meals I want to make for my family that week and the other is the grocery list (which I may have already started – we keep one on the refrigerator and I've trained the husband and kiddo to add things to it when we run out). I page through sales flyers and make my shopping list, double-checking my refrigerator, freezer and pantry to see if I need any of the items that are on sale.

Clean up after every meal

Cleaning up after yourself only takes a moment or two, and keeps your kitchen clean (less attractive to pests) and ready for you to prepare your next meal. It is the little things, a glass here and a plate there, that add up to a large amount of clutter very quickly.

After eating, rinse your dishes and place them in the dishwasher, wipe down your counters and put away any food. In just a few minutes of work your kitchen is now ready and waiting for the next meal.

Note: in late 2017, our dishwasher died. The motor needed to be replaced. Now we had already had a run of bad luck in regards to appliances, so I was pretty frustrated. I decided I didn't need a new dishwasher and we have been handwashing our dishes ever since.

I have found that, if I clean the dishes right after a meal, and wash the pots and pans as I go when cooking, my kitchen is now pristine clean AND I don't ever have to wait for the dishwasher to finish washing my dishes. Less energy expenditure, it is done in about the same time as it would take me to rinse off the dishes and load them into the machine, and my counters and sink stay sparkling clean!

Bathrooms

<u>While You Are Waiting</u>

While you are waiting for your water to heat, keep yourself busy. This is a great time to organize! Try doing some (or all) of the following each day:

- Put away items on the counter in the cabinets and drawers where they belong
- Spritz the mirror with glass cleaner and wipe it down
- Re-stock the toilet rolls for ease of access
- Quick rinse your sink free of dirt and hair

<u>Discard, Evaluate and Combine</u>

How many empty or nearly empty bottles are in your shower? In the years that I ran a housecleaning service I was amazed at just how many clients had empty bottles still sitting in their showers and bathtubs. It actually makes sense, it isn't as if you have a trash can right there and you are in the middle of showering so you can't just step over to the trash can and throw the empty bottle away. Personally I just set the empty container outside on the bathmat and then throw it away once I have finished my shower.

Regularly look over the items in your medicine cabinet, on your sink and below—are you using these items? Remove soaps that irritate or dry your skin, give away or throw out toiletries that you don't use and toss out non-functioning curling irons, etc.

If you have multiples of the same shampoo or body wash, combine them into one container. This reduces clutter.

<u>Set a Cleaning Schedule</u>

Bathrooms need regular cleaning to prevent the spread of mold and bacteria. I advise cleaning a bathroom once every other week. The shower or bathtub is easy, clean it while you are in it! Clean your mirrors, dust, sanitize your toilet while you are waiting for your water to heat or give the sink a quick scrub.

Home Office

<u>While You Are Waiting</u>

While you are waiting for your computer to boot:

- Tidy your desk
- Sift through any items in your 'in' box
- Shred paper from your 'Shred' box
- Clean your monitor, keyboard or mouse

<u>File It Now</u>

Don't put off your filing for later. As you process your mail, and pay a bill, file it immediately. Your filing cabinet should be located as close to your desk and computer as possible for ease in filing.

Front Entry/Coat Closet

When I return home after a day spent organizing and cleaning, my toddler comes running to greet me. I have only a few seconds before she insists that I pick her up and hold her.

It would be easy for me to simply dump everything I am holding (purse, papers, etc.) into a heap on the floor and reach down and pick her up. Instead, I take just a few seconds and put away my purse on a shelf in the hall closet, hang up my coat and then pick up my daughter and hold her as I deliver my work papers to the 'in' box in my office.

A few seconds now, means minutes saved later—I don't have to track down my cell phone or keys that my little one would later ransack from the purse left on the floor—and I won't have to extricate any crumpled work papers from her hands either.

Even if you don't have an inquisitive toddler, take a few seconds to organize your mobile life with your fixed one and put away the items you bring into the house.

Bedrooms

<u>When You Wake Up</u>

- Make your bed
- Let in the light
- Tidy up

I'll be honest here—my bed gets made about 50% of the time (and that's being generous). My husband and I often forget, and I tend to be out of bed and moving an hour before he even wakes up, so we often don't make the bed. That said—it feels wonderful to walk into my bedroom in the evening and slip the covers back on a neatly made bed. There's something truly relaxing about it. If you don't normally make your bed, try it, just for a week, and see how it feels. For some it may feel like just one more thing to do, but for others it will be well worth the small amount of effort.

Open up your curtains and let in the light. Even if you are not a morning person like me, sunlight revives our energy levels and illuminates our days. It can help you jump-start your morning! It will also help bring your attention to any mess that needs to be tidied up.

If you left your clothes in a heap by the side of the bed, pick them up and toss them in the laundry basket. If you had any dirty dishes (glass of milk before bed, etc.) pick them up and 'stage them' by setting them close to the door to go out or just go ahead and take them to the kitchen, whichever works best for you.

I jump into the shower as soon as I wake up, so I usually leave any dirty dishes on top of my dresser near the door. When I'm showered and dressed I grab them and head for the kitchen to brew my morning coffee.

<u>Before You Go To Sleep</u>

- Tidy up
- Start a list

Before going to bed, take a moment to pick up books or dirty dishes in your bedroom and 'stage' them near the exit. Toss your clothes into the laundry basket or hang them up if you plan on wearing them again.

I keep a list near my bed and add all kinds of notes:

- *Buy milk*
- *Vacuum tomorrow*
- *Call Mom re: trip*
- *Order flea meds for dogs*

It serves as a jump-start to my day the next morning and means I don't have to get up and go do the task 'right this minute.'

Living Rooms

Model good habits to your children and your spouse by tidying up the living room each evening before bedtime. Straighten the couch cushions, pick up dirty dishes and bus them to the kitchen sink and put any books or magazines back in order.

When you return to the living room the next day, it will feel so much more welcoming!

Closets

Maintain order by separating hangers in use from empty hangers. As you take down a shirt or dress, place the empty hanger to one side. That way you aren't searching for hangers later with an armful of clean laundry to hang. They are there to one side, waiting to be used again.

Plan on re-visiting your closets twice per year. Weed out any clothing you have ceased wearing. After you have established a regular pattern, it will take mere minutes to go through your closets—so don't procrastinate, you will only make the job longer and more arduous by delaying!

Time Management

Perhaps you have noticed that you have a poor sense of time and are often late for appointments, late for work and children are late for school.

This often occurs because of inability to find misplaced items, distractions, and an unrealistic sense of how long a task will take to complete. Following are some ideas that will help with these issues as well as other time saving tips.

Plan

Plan your morning the night before: lay out the clothes you will wear, gather your briefcase, and collect the children's clothes, backpacks, shoes and items needed to take to school. Think through everything you will need in the morning and have that ready to go. Request and encourage your school-age children to do this nightly to avoid morning madness.

When planning errands, be realistic about the amount of time each errand will take. Add *at least* 15 minutes to the time you think it will take. This way you will learn not to over schedule and continually work under pressure.

Organize

Find a secure place by the door or entry to household to hang or hold your keys. Several ideas are in catalogs or you may find key holders in organizing stores. This space or area may also be a place where outgoing mail and other outgoing items are kept. A nice basket in the area works well.

Maintain a family message center and a perpetual shopping list.

Schedule

Schedule your priority tasks early in the week so if they have to be displaced there is still time left to complete them. Also schedule the most difficult tasks during your "prime time" when you are at peak energy level. Recognize that you do not have to complete the entire job in one sitting. Do a little at a time by scheduling appointments with yourself and keeping them.

Prioritize

Remember that you are procrastinating if you work on a trivial task while a more important one remains undone. Prioritize the jobs to be done and work on priorities first.

In Summary

You purchased this book with the hopes that it would get you organized once and for all. And in the preceding sections we have discussed not only how to become organized and stay that way, but also how the clutter came to add up in the first place.

As I said in the introductions I don't have any magic answer for you. What I have given you is, quite simply, good advice on:

- Understanding the roots of clutter
- An invitation to examine your spending and shopping habits closely
- Basic and advanced organizing tips
- How to get motivated and stay that way
- Techniques for staying organized once you conquered clutter in your living space

As I said earlier, I deeply believe that the infinite capacity for change is within all of us. If you want to be organized strongly enough, you *can* make it happen. You can do this by putting into practice the suggestions and techniques in this book.

It is estimated that it takes 21 days of practice to make a particular action into a habit. Don't you think it's time to start making some good habits?

I welcome your comments or questions. I may be reached by email: shuckchristine@gmail.com.

Happy Organizing!

| Page

Section 4: Resources

| Page

Whether you are looking for a professional organizer to help get you started, or organizations to take your stuff, here are a few resources I have found to be very helpful. I have categorized them by type.

Donations

Goodwill Industries, Inc.
    http://www.goodwill.org
    (800) 741-0186
    Salvation Army
    http://www.salvationarmyusa.org
    1-800-728-7825
    Big Brothers/Big Sisters
    http://www.bbbs.org
    (215) 567-7000 (National headquarters in PA)
    Freecycle
    www.freecycle.org[1]

---

1.   http://www.freecycle.org

Professional Organizations

National Association of Professional Organizers– NAPO
   http://www.napo.net/
   National Study Group on Chronic Disorganization – NGSCD
   http://www.nsgcd.org/
   Professional Organizers Web Ring – POWR
   http://www.organizerswebring.com/

Organizing Advice

FlyLady
  http://www.flylady.net/
  Online Organizing.com
  http://www.onlineorganizing.com/Home.asp

Hauling Services

Got Junk?
  http://www.1800gotjunk.com
  1-800-GOTJUNK

Open-Source Software

Accounting:
http://www.roseindia.net/opensource/
open-source-accounting-software.shtml

Author's Note

Thanks for reading, I hope you found it useful. I would be grateful if you could post a review of this book on Goodreads or your favorite go-to location for reviewing books. Put simply, reviews show that others have read the book and found it worth their time.

So...do you like to read for free? I know, I already asked you that once, but just in case, I figured I would ask you again. Forgive me, I've been told I am rather persistent at times. It's a fault, I know, however...

Sign up for my newsletter and each month you will receive a handy dandy "tip of the month" that can help jumpstart your organizing, or keep it in shape after you have finished reading this book.

No obligation to make any future purchases or anything else like that.

Also, you will also have access to a brand-new, short story set within the Kapalaran Universe. You can learn more about the Kapalaran Universe at my website: http://christineshuck.com

I promise to:

Never sell/share your email address
Never push you to buy my other books
Make unsubscribing as easy as pushing a button.

Interested?   Great!   Join   the   newsletter   list   here:
https://mailchi.mp/c05ceb84e66a/subscribe-me

Don't go away yet, here is the first chapter from my non-fiction book *The War on Drugs: An Old Wives Tale...*

Excerpt From The War On Drugs: An Old Wives Tale – the tale of one family's

Excerpt: A Beginning and an End

I met my husband Dave in 1984-in our sophomore year of high school. We both attended a small, private high school in San Francisco. The first year of school we spent together, we were lost in our own shy little worlds. He barely spoke to anyone-and chewed nervously on his jacket strings. I had been there a year, but I too was painfully shy. I would remain this way into my early 20s. When I dared to speak, it was to other outcasts like him-who were safe and friendly. By the end of that first year together, we had begun sitting at the same table and a quiet friendship had developed..

We were friends, just friends. However, as we headed into our junior year and we both began to grow out of our shells; I realized quite painfully that I was head over heels for this friendly, kind, and good-looking boy. I became one of a group of girls who spent an inordinate amount of time watching the boys play hacky sack in front of the large picture window during recess and lunch. Many of them were the 'popular' kids, and Dave stood on the outskirts of this group, still merging with my friends, but now spending his weekends with the other group at parties.

Much to my regret, our friendship during that time never progressed past the friend stage. After high school, I moved south to

San Jose and got married, and soon after had a baby. A few years later that marriage ended disastrously. I connected with Dave once in 1995, invited him to dinner, but he was engaged to be married and made the appropriate excuses. Again, we lost touch. In 1997, I moved to Missouri, met and married another disaster and we divorced in early 2002. I was still licking my wounds from that experience when Dave discovered me on Classmates.com.

A few days before Christmas in 2002, he sent me an email wishing me a Merry Christmas and asking me how my life was. Sixteen years after high school and I felt like a teenager all over again, with butterflies in my stomach and love-struck eyes. My teenage daughter was very amused at my transformation.

After all, he was 'the one that got away.' I had never had the guts in high school to say to his face, "I like you, a lot. Now would you please go out with me?" Over the years, whenever I would connect with old classmates I would always ask, "Have you heard from Dave Shuck? How is he?" Even then, I knew my voice gave me away. I was too interested, too desperate for news. The memory of him stayed with me, haunting me. He had been the first boy I had ever fallen for, hard, and I looked for him in other men's faces and in their smiles.

A thousand times I had regretted never telling him how I felt. It felt like an unfinished story. Yet here I was, 1,500 miles away, half a lifetime later, and it felt like high school all over again. We exchanged emails. We shared hours of long, soulful, amusing, reminiscent phone calls. He had been divorced for four years, no children, and I was rebounding from a traumatizing divorce and struggling to make ends meet as a single mom to my now-teenage daughter. Finally, after two weeks of nearly daily phone calls he admitted that he had been terribly disappointed to learn I was no longer in California. "I was going to ask you out on a date," he said.

"What's 1,500 miles between friends?" I said, sounding far more confident than I felt. "I'd love to go to dinner with you. Come and see me, Dave." He laughed at first, but I repeated the offer, and then repeated it again. To my delight and terror, that is just what he did.

In late January 2003, he flew out for a week. It was unseasonably cold; the temperatures plunged to minus 10 degrees Fahrenheit, cold enough that my bathroom pipes froze and burst. I fell on the ice one morning and hurt my back. I spent the day on the couch in a haze of pain while he located the busted pipe in an unheated crawl space off of the main basement and helped the plumber repair it.

Before he left at the end of the week I said, "We're good people who have had plenty of awful things happen to us. We deserve some good. I'd like you to stay with me." Dropping him off at the airport and watching him fly away was one of the most difficult things I have ever done. I sobbed as I drove home. I knew I loved him still, that I had never really stopped loving him, not after all those years.

Some part of him must have felt the same way because two months later he packed up and drove to Missouri. He left behind all of his family and friends in San Francisco, the only place he had ever lived, to be with me. That was March of 2003.

It was tough finding a job at first. He did a couple of stints with bottom of the barrel call center positions before landing a job in the computer field as a repairs technician working with industrial computers. Here he stayed while I quit my job, started my own business, and went back to school part-time. Six weeks into my first semester at UMKC, we learned I was pregnant. We married July 2, 2006 and our daughter P.E. was born October 4, 2006.

I could not have asked for a better father or husband. Dave was and still is committed, loving, and attentive. He has loved our little girl since the moment he saw her there on the ultrasound, snoozing inside me, and he was lost from the moment he first held her in his arms. I say this because I want it understood that, mistakes or not, or poor judgment on either of our parts, we are a family. We love each other deeply. When the proverbial crap hits the fan, we gather in, pull the edges away from the world, and center on what is important – our little family.

Computers had lost their allure long ago, but Dave stayed at his job. He stuck it out there for over four years before he found himself laid off at the end of May 2008. The fact that he had stayed in a job that he had come to despise, so that we would continue to have a dependable income and health insurance was a price he had been more than willing to pay. However, I had seen how it had pushed him into depression and constant anxiety as he fought to stay focused in a field he no longer loved and in a job where he was degraded daily.

When the ax fell, I was actually relieved. "Take a month, even two or three," I told him. "You'll get unemployment and you need a break. Maybe now you can take some time for yourself and figure out what you want to do going forward." We tightened our belts, reduced our expenditures where we could, and turned our attention to family and home. I began working more hours with my cleaning business and at the professional organizing business I had started in 2007. I finished writing my first book on organizing and published it myself.

Two weeks after he lost his job Dave said, "I want to start a microbrewery and brew craft beer."

Brew beer? I don't even like the stuff. I can barely manage a sip or two out of politeness. But if that was what he wanted, then I would do what I could to make it happen. "Okay," I said. "Let's open a brewery."

Small problem ... money. Or, more specifically, a serious lack thereof.

It was my bright idea that helped build the walls which would later crash down on top of us. "Let's finish the basement out, create a secret room in it and grow marijuana," I suggested. "We can sell it and make enough money in a few years to come up with what we need to start the brewery."

In writing the paragraph above, I recall a television show, *Weeds*, which I watched obsessively for several seasons. The main character,

Nancy Botwin, found herself a widow with no money and no real work skills, so she turned to selling dime bags of pot to make ends meet. One disaster after another, season after season, this woman's whole life was a hot mess. By the time Dave entered drug court, Nancy Botwin had set fire to her giant house in the suburbs, set metaphorical fires to most of her relationships, had a baby out of wedlock, and married her Mexican crime lord baby daddy. I just couldn't stop watching it – it was like a train wreck you can't tear your eyes away from.

We are not an episode of *Weeds*. I am not Nancy Botwin. Yet for a moment, looking at those words that I uttered, *"Let's finish the basement out, create a secret room in it and grow marijuana,"* it all seems so ridiculous, so completely asinine that now, I cannot believe I suggested we do it.

But I did suggest it, and Dave agreed to do it. We finished out the basement and created the secret room, dubbed 'Ground Zero' by the police. We bought the lights, rockwool, bags of Miracle Gro and all kinds of high-end fertilizers. Everything we needed to promote growth, encourage flowering, and eventually grow enormous buds of sticky, stinky, money-making, stupor-inducing splendor. We put in an air conditioner to reduce the high temperatures caused by the bright lights, a carbon filter and an ionizer to reduce smell. After a few months, we managed to reduce the smell to the immediate area, where no one but us would have reason to venture. We even entertained guests during this time-*non-smoking* guests, that is.

Nearly all of our family and friends are non-smokers. Dave, on the other hand, had been smoking since he was a teenager. He had only stopped once he moved to Missouri due to the lack of a good connection or high-quality product. My husband can be a bit of a snob at times. He enjoys micro-brewed beer and expensive, high-end weed. As for me, I am a writer, with a strong, type-A personality. I run two businesses of my own, help Dave with his business and typically have a smorgasbord of household, craft, and writing projects underway simultaneously. Smoking weed interfered with all of my commitments. When high I cease to be able to operate simple machinery, such as a microwave, and my productivity comes to a screeching halt. My internal barriers, thin as they already are, come down and I say whatever is on my mind, inevitably embarrassing or harsh. I don't like how it makes me feel, so my sampling of the product was, and still is, a rare and unusual occurrence.

We made a very nice, high-end weed come out of our basement. Kush and White Widow; both strains were mild tasting yet strong. They easily sold at a price of $4,000 per pound, no haggling, and no problems.

Before I get too far, I also want to dispel the notion that we actually made *money* at this enterprise, because in the end, we lost thousands of dollars. When it all shook out, we probably made one dollar for every ten dollars we lost. Thousands of dollars in equipment were lost on the day of the raid, and we paid at least $30,000 more in raised utility bills, lawyer fees, and court costs before it all shook out.

This is also not some kind of a treatise on how the system 'done us wrong,' nor is it intended as a forum to brag about our law-breaking ways. It is an account of how we, Dave and I, became involved in the production of marijuana, how we were caught, and what happened afterwards. If it causes you to question the 'system' or wag your finger at your kids as a warning of what happens to 'those kind of people,' that is your decision. Think what you want, believe what you care to believe; learn what you will from our lessons ... if there even is one.

I also need to make clear how *long* growing marijuana takes when you are first starting out. Some of the seeds took forever to sprout, the germination rate was horrendous, and I began to wonder how old the seeds we used were. We were hit with a host of other problems ... heat issues, smell issues, male plants (very bad) and finally, these small flies that ate our delicate plants from the root up. Our harvests, when they occurred, were sad, pitiful affairs and the electric bill quickly doubled.

By November 2008 we had managed one and a half good harvests, with maybe two to two and a half pounds of dried product. We had finally figured out a cycle of cloning, learned to control our pest problem, and were about to clone a new batch when disaster struck.

It was less than a week before Thanksgiving 2008 and we had just moved out our first real harvest of product to the buyer. We had paid some bills and had cash stashed away. Not a lot of cash, but enough to get by for a while. Dave had just returned with a brand new set of lights that promised to conserve energy while making those money-making plants grow like mad. A friend was visiting; he was going to help us with painting in return for Dave's help re-wiring parts of his house the week before. We walked outside to unload the lights when three black SUVs screeched to a halt in front of our house. One pulled in behind our friend's truck, the other behind our van, and the third blocked the entire exit to the driveway.

A tall bald guy came striding up to my husband and said, "Dave Shuck? Still running a cleaning business out of your home?" He said it with a sneer, as if he was sure the answer was "no." We later learned that people use things like cleaning businesses as a front for laundering drug money. I actually did own and run a housecleaning business at that time. For that matter, I still do.

My husband must have nodded or said something in the affirmative in response to the officer's question, but mainly he was staring in horror at the badge the guy was flashing. "Well, I've got bad news for you, Dave. We've come for your plants."

Dave turned to me and said, "Honey, I'm going to prison." I love my husband, I really do, but I had forgotten how he was wired – tell the truth and obey police at all times. In this situation, it was suboptimal. His response was a dead giveaway that we were up to exactly what they were hoping we were.

The bald man stepped closer, as did the other men, ringing my husband and cutting me off from him. They focused on him as their main target, honing in on him as the weaker link in this situation. The head guy made a broad gesture, pointing toward the other middle-class houses and manicured lawns that surrounded us on all sides, "Let us in and your neighbors don't have to know that anything is wrong. We are not going to call DFS and we are not going to arrest you. We just want your plants." He smiled, "We'll be in and out of here in less than an hour."

I would like to think that I would have handled it differently. I know that the 'coulda woulda, shoulda' scenarios haunted me as they ran through my mind for weeks and months afterwards. I kept imagining how I would have stood my ground and acted confused. Maybe backed up fast, gone inside, and locked the door behind me. I could have asked for their warrant, or even told them to get off my property. Something, *anything* but say what Dave had said. I would have tried to buy us enough time to clear everything out. It would not have been that hard. If they had come by a few days earlier, they would have caught us with at least one pound of marijuana dried and ready for sale. If they had come by a few days later, they would have caught us with 48 new clones.

That day in November was the start of a surreal world we would find ourselves in over the next two years. My husband, terrified beyond measure at the thought of losing our child to DFS, had signed a form allowing them to enter our house and showed them the grow room. He did this without reading what he was signing or asking if they had a warrant. By the time I thought to ask if they had a warrant, they had already been inside the house and seen the grow room. The man in charge, Jay Flight, said, "No, we don't. If we need to get that, we can. We will return with a DFS worker and I can't promise you won't be arrested."

I nodded, "I understand your threat; go ahead with what you are doing."

He smiled, "It's not a threat."

In my world, when you say that you will bring in the Department of Family Services and imply that there could be arrests, you are threatening me. However, the point was irrelevant; it was far too late for me to do anything but cooperate.

We learned quickly, albeit too late, that it had been a simple fishing expedition. What the police refer to as a "knock and talk." They had been staking out a hydroponics store in Kansas City for nearly a year. They followed Dave from the hydroponics store that day after they observed him purchasing the high-intensity grow lights. We were just another pair of fish hooked by the Clandestine Lab Task Force. After entering the drug court program, Dave would meet many more snared in the exact the same way.

They took pictures, video even, then photographed and fingerprinted both of us. They bagged up the plants to send to the lab. As we watched the process, the head guy, Jay Flight, smiled at us, "I know, I know, it's kind of like getting your kids taken away from you." We both just looked at him and shook our heads.

"No, it isn't. Our daughter is upstairs and she is our child. These plants mean nothing to us compared to her." I said, wondering for the first, but not the last, time just what kind of people he was used to dealing with. Dave made noises of agreement behind me.

They did not arrest us that day, a fact for which I am very grateful. I would learn later that cops can and will lie to you and say whatever it takes to get your cooperation. They can make grandiose promises, pledging to not call Child Protective Services, the media, or arrest you, and then later do exactly that. We were lucky; they kept their promises that day and left with only the plants and the thousands of dollars in equipment and lights. We sat there, contemplated running like hell for the border, hugged our daughter, and tried to figure out what to do next.

The task force had removed 13 plants, ten of which were scraggly and sad, on the point of death, and less than 1/8 of an ounce of weed.

They missed our stash of cash, but then again, they had not looked too hard for that. Mainly they were interested in the high-end equipment, the lights still in their boxes, and anything they could confiscate and immediately sell.

Long before the results were back from the lab and the warrant issued for Dave's arrest, Flight's group had sold our confiscated property at a police auction. I learned later that every penny of that money went back to fund the task force and that, in the case of this particular task force, there is little oversight or restrictions on how they spent that money. This is probably why they all drive sleek black SUVs and look so well dressed. No matter how the charges had played out against us, they would never have to return or even pay for the property they had confiscated.

Yes, I will admit it. It galls me. Essentially, it is legal thievery hidden behind that nondescript legal term – "asset forfeiture." Even if they never charged us, even if the lab tests had come back negative, they would not have had to return the equipment or reimburse us in any way. If they had found cash on the premises, it would have been up to us to prove that the money was ours legitimately (i.e., *not* drug money). The potential for abuse through asset forfeiture is extraordinary and I will discuss this in more detail later.

It is an incontrovertible fact that the War on Drugs is wrapped tightly around the issue of money. This task force, and its brothers in law enforcement, uses Asset Foreclosure as an excuse to confiscate belongings and cash from hundreds of thousands of people each year. Many of these people have not broken the law, but they still lose. If I hadn't already been convinced of this fact, I certainly was months after the raid as we were cleaning up the house in anticipation of visits by trackers-a type of police officer whose job it is to search drug court participants' homes and cars for illicit substances. We rented a storage unit to house the banned items, such as Dave's beer brewing system, our beer glass collection, beer T-shirts, memorabilia, and books on beer making. If these items had remained in our immediate home, they would have been subject to confiscation and eventual sale.

As we cleared out the basement, I noticed that the task force had left behind part of the hydroponics system. I pointed it out to Dave, remarking that it was strange they had not taken it. "They said it wasn't worth any money, so they weren't going to bother taking it." My husband explained. I did not believe him and said so. "Seriously," he insisted, "*they said* they wouldn't be able to get anything for it when they sold it so they left it."

This is what I mean when I say that the War on Drugs is more about making money and less about protecting people from the dangers of drugs. If the issue is to discourage people from producing drugs by confiscating the production equipment used, then that crappy little piece of plastic that a row of plants sat in should have been confiscated along with the other items. The fact that it, along with other items that had no 'resale value,' were left behind speaks very loudly to drug task force priorities – get it, grab what you can make money off of, and move on. It is not about stopping crime, it is about *making money*.

In the week following the bust, we had found a lawyer and set an appointment. Our defense attorney was an ex-prosecutor, and his partner was an ex-drug cop. During our meeting the ex-drug cop was playing with his new wireless camera. He would wink at me and tell me to "smile for the camera." It seems that old habits die hard with cops; I was far from amused.

They advised us to have our cars detailed. When we looked confused they explained, "Pot smokers smoke in their cars." We shook our heads and told them we never did. "Well, you might transport pot in your car then." Again, we shook our heads no, that we never had. The two of them looked at each other, eyebrows raised, and I could tell they were not sure whether to believe us or not. If I could have seen inside their heads then I am sure there would have been a vision of two stoned idiots driving down the road, smoking a joint with our young child looking on from the backseat. Nothing could have been further from the truth.

They told us it would be $7,500 to represent both of us. We scrounged up $3,000 and agreed to begin making regular payments of $100 per month. Then we went home and, after P.E. was asleep, smoked the pot missed by the task force. By that point, my stress levels were so high that I indulged as well.

One week later, we began taking regular urine tests. Our lawyer advised us to do this. He hoped to be able to prove that the marijuana was for personal use only and indicated that we were clean or getting that way. I had smoked recently, several times shortly after the raid, and Dave had been smoking heavily for months. All of this was outside or in the garage, away from our daughter and usually after she was in bed for the night. We kept it away from her always, and to this day she has no idea what marijuana is or what a marijuana pipe looks like, as she has never seen it in use.

I say this because I want you to have a clear picture of our life. Ours is a middle-class home in a middle-class neighborhood where the biggest excitement had been a recent rash of break-ins when people were away at work. We have extensive flower gardens and raise fresh herbs and okra, squash and asparagus each summer. We are the people next door who always have a spare cup of sugar or an extra egg. I am in the habit of bringing fresh-baked cookies to new neighbors, and we swap recipes and gardening advice. For us, the worst thing you will see is a few days of rather long grass (that would be our *lawn,* not *marijuana*) when we are caught up in other projects. In other words, we are normal people, with decent cars; a well-cared-for child, and great neighbors in a quiet suburb south of Kansas City.

The marijuana cleared out of my system quickly. In less than a month, I was as clean as a whistle. Dave took longer, nearly three months to be exact. This was exactly what the lawyer had hoped for. Although the number of plants was enough to put us in the production category instead of just personal consumption, the party line had to be that we were growing it for personal use. "Look, see here, big time pot smoker, used to smoking a lot. He's from California, for Christ sake!" Which is not to say that everyone in California is a pothead, but let's face it: things are a little different out there and it was a good defense.

The lawyer advised us to enroll in a drug-counseling program. We went to Pathways and enrolled. We each had different counselors. After the initial assessment, my counselor advised that my program would entail ten individual therapy sessions and ten group therapy sessions. This meant I had to drive down to Harrisonville each week to see her, but I could go to the closer town of Raymore to attend the group sessions.

My one-on-one counselor was serious and rather dour at first as I struggled with the material she presented to me. In particular, I struggled with the idea that any repeated use over any length of time is addiction. I simply could not agree with this premise. At one point, early on in our meetings I stopped in the middle of the exercise and asked, "After this many weeks I hope you will believe me when I say that I smoke pot rarely, if ever. Now here I am in this position – waiting to hear when we will face charges and whether there will be the possibility of prison. Surely you have met someone in my position before this."

She shook her head, "Never. Not once. And I've been doing this for 30 years." It blew me away. It also did set a new, altered tone for our meetings. As my story remained the same, and did not crack or reveal inconsistencies, I think she came to realize that I was telling the truth. Most of our subsequent visits were less tense and at times, even friendly, as I shared with her my impressions of the group sessions and the other attendees. She laughed when I compared attending group counseling to an interesting social experiment. Months later, when Dave began the drug court program, he would relay that the individuals in the Pathways group sessions were college professors in comparison with the drug court participants.

One particular encounter with this counselor stayed with me, however. It was our third or fourth scheduled meeting and I had been participating in a class online and then had to race down to Harrisonville.

I was running late, just five minutes or so, but I called and let the secretary know I was on my way. When I arrived my counselor met me at the door with a sour look and said in a very confrontational manner, "If you are ever late for one of our meetings again I will discontinue your treatment. The state requires you to meet with me for the full 45 minutes and not a minute less. Do you understand?"

I was tempted to walk out right then, but I was quite aware that these meetings might eventually help our case, so I apologized and then waited for her to escort me to her office. No regular counselor would have ever spoken to me like that. She did it in as rude and confrontational manner as she possibly could. Combine that with the fact that she regularly started our sessions five minutes late and ended our sessions at precisely one half hour (15 minutes short of the "mandated meeting length") at nearly *every visit*, I saw her behavior as hypocritical, petty, and controlling.

She was telling me quite clearly that she was in charge and I had better toe the line. This type of behavior is endemic in the law enforcement and drug treatment world. I made note of each departure time from there on out – we never once met for a full 45 minutes. The way I see it, when you won't follow your own rules, you forfeit all respect for your authority. Her behavior was nothing more than posturing and a play for power.

The waiting stretched out interminably. Our lawyer told us that the laboratory that had received our plants was very behind in processing. So much so that it was late May before the tests came back positive for marijuana and a warrant issued. On May 26, 2009, they issued a warrant for Dave's arrest. Until that point, we had assumed they would charge us both. Instead they pursued charges against only Dave.

Despite this, I would not breathe easy until a full year had elapsed. In our county, the authorities have 12 months to charge an individual after discovering that a crime has been committed. I would later learn that Dave had begged the task force not to pursue charges against me. He told them that, while I had known about it, I had not participated in any part of the marijuana growing operation. This was partially true. He was in charge of cultivation and harvests, but I had been in charge of the finances.

His assuming the blame would enable us to survive the two years that would follow. If we had both been in drug court, we would have lost all possible income, our house, and any chance of maintaining a stable home and family life for our daughter during that time.

Although the court issued the warrant on May 26th, our lawyer did not learn of it until June 12th. He called us that Friday afternoon and advised Dave to keep his head down for the weekend. He also arranged for Dave to turn himself in on the Monday after Father's Day, post bond, and be released pending trial that same day.

Father's Day weekend was a mess; we were both terrified. The hammer had come down. I talked Dave into going out to a Father's Day lunch at Flying Saucer, a beer bar in the newly revitalized Kansas City Power & Light district. Neither of us knew what might happen the next day and we were worried and scared. All we knew was that the charges were for a Class B felony, intent to manufacture and distribute a controlled substance. It carried with it a possible sentence of five to 15 years. As frightened as we both were, I knew that I needed to give him some semblance of normalcy. We went to lunch, enjoyed the day as best we could, and cuddled up close in bed that evening.

One note of interest to the reader: of the 13 plants that the team had seized, only ten of them were reported. Keep in mind, ten of these plants had already been harvested and were scraggly and dying. We had kept them on hand to see if we could manage to wring a few clones out of the worn-out leaves while other three plants (the ones *not* listed in the team's report) were the healthy ones all set to be cloned into new plants. What ever happened to the other three plants? You can bet that neither of us decided to mention that discrepancy. I will leave it to you, the reader, to make up your own mind on how or why that discrepancy might have occurred or where those three plants ended up.

Our lawyer was still talking about drug court being an option, but was careful not to make grandiose promises – there was still the very real possibility that Dave could go to prison. On Monday morning, I drove him down to the county seat, dropped him off, and went to pull money out of the bank to cover bail. The bail had been set at $7,500 and the lawyer was able to negotiate with the court to allow us to post 10% of it directly to the courts. Five hours and $750 later, Dave was free on bond. Our next court date was set for July 20, 2009.

His brief few hours in jail were stressful for him and frightening when he related them to me. It took nearly two hours to process him in, with one of the officers, Good Ole Boy, taunting, "Oh, I surrender! I surrender!" in a falsetto before putting him into a holding cell with three other men. "Now don't tell them about those cigarettes I let you keep!" He walked away laughing.

The men inside looked Dave up and down and one asked, "You holding?"

"Holding what?"

"Cigarettes, asshole. Are you holding?"

Dave gestured at his empty pockets, "I don't even smoke cigarettes."

"Yeah, but are you *holding*?" When Dave continued to look confused the man clarified, "Do you have them up your *ass*?" When Dave said no, the man winked at the others, "Maybe we should search you anyway."

Never having been in the system, we both realized later they may have just been giving Dave a hard time, razzing him a bit to keep themselves amused while they waited. However, some of the crimes these men had committed were rather terrifying. The one that stands out, even now, was the man who took a pickax to a man who had, as he told Dave, "disrespected my woman while I was in the joint." A *pickax*...good Lord, we had entered a world filled with madmen.

By the end of the waiting, he had been called a cream puff, and the others had grinned as they commented how much they hoped he could have a sleepover with them that night.

The guards were just as bad, barking orders, engaging in little power plays and intimidation tactics that would have shamed their mothers. I still ask myself, who were the worse animals, the ones with the keys or the ones behind bars? One side had no power, and they were being reminded of this fact, repeatedly. As a result, the moment they had a chance, they acted out. The other side had the power, and used it, and abused it, *because they could.*

More than ever I was determined to keep Dave out of jail. This was not the place for him. Running like hell for the border was even discussed. "Whatever it takes," I promised him, "we will keep you out of that place."

Three weeks of agonized waiting. Our lawyer had promised to contact us as soon as he had heard from the prosecutor, but he heard nothing. We went into court on July 20th completely blind. Would they tell us that drug court was out of the question? Would they reduce the charge down to a Class C felony (simple possession)? Would the drug task force object to drug court as our lawyer believed they would?

I told my mother we both had meetings to attend and arranged for her to keep P.E. for a long weekend. We dropped her off on Sunday afternoon and returned home, putting the house in order and distracting ourselves with mundane tasks such as laundry and mowing.

We waited anxiously for our lawyer outside of the courtroom, not realizing he was inside. When he did come out, he had surprising news for us. "The task force has given the thumbs up for you to attend drug court," he said.

"What?" I said. "I thought you said that never happens."

Our lawyer, who had extensive experience with other marijuana-growing operations the task force had busted, shook his head and said, "In all of my experience, in all of my years as a prosecutor and now as a defense attorney, they have *never* agreed to a recommendation for drug court. You are the first I've ever heard of."

Having the drug task force disagree with a recommendation for drug court was the norm, which didn't carry a huge amount of weight, since plenty of others had been admitted despite the task force's objections, but it was unusual. It was one of the many indicators we would have that our case was unusual from others in many crucial ways. It also gave me hope, albeit foolish and quickly dashed hope, that Dave's experience in drug court would somehow be easier as a result. It was not, but we would remain the anomaly in many ways throughout our drug court experience.

Dave went before the judge and the charges were read. The judge's eyebrows shot up when the prosecutor stated that the drug task force had no objections to drug court. It wasn't just a surprise to our lawyer, but to the judge as well. The result of that day in court meant an *opportunity* to possibly participate in drug court. Dave was instructed to meet with Sherrie, the coordinator for the program, to discuss his possible participation, as soon as possible.

Our lawyer explained the process of qualifying for drug court and advised Dave, "When you meet with Sherrie, simply explain that although you have been drug-free since November, *remaining drug-free from your addiction*," he took care to put special emphasis on those words, "continues to be a struggle for you, something you have to work at one day at a time."

We went home and Dave made an appointment to meet Sherrie first thing in the morning. The next day he went to his meeting and I dashed off to two cleanings and back home to prepare to teach an organizing class that night. As I got ready, Dave deluged me with details about his meeting. There was a laundry list of prohibited items that would have to be removed from the house and put in storage.

Prohibited items included any brewing equipment, any beer glasses, T-shirts, or other beer paraphernalia. No Sudafed, Nyquil, prescription pain medication or alcohol of any kind, including mouthwash, was allowed.

Phase One of the program would be the most difficult. Sherrie explained that he would be required to call in to a hotline each day to find out the color of the day. His color would be green. How appropriate! Anytime the color of the day was designated green, he would need to report to either the sheriff's department or to an officer of the drug court and submit to a drug test.

He would be required to attend the drug court diversion program every day of the week except Wednesday and Sunday and he would also be expected to attend Narcotics Anonymous meetings three times a week. On his free days it was entirely likely he would also be called to perform community service on an as-needed basis. Phase One would last a minimum of eight weeks and during that time the drug court did not want Dave to have any kind of employment at all.

Dave was instructed by Sherrie to clear everything out of our house that was drug or alcohol-related. When it was all out of the house she would do a walk-through. We rented a storage facility and moved it all out. The year before when we were planning on starting a brewery we bought a 20 gallon professional grade brew system for R&D purposes.

When we learned prior to starting the drug court program that prohibited equipment was subject to confiscation if not removed from the premises, we immediately moved it to the storage unit. Thirty dollars a month for storage was a small price to pay for almost $10,000 in equipment.

Dave called the phone number Sherrie had given him and let her know we were ready. She was a small, muscular woman with the sharp, no-nonsense attitude I've seen in policewomen. Beneath the muted makeup and conservative hairstyle lay the steely resolve that propels them through the police academy and into a profession dominated by men. Dave had mentioned that she had served as a patrolwoman before transferring into the probation department.

She gave a cursory onceover of the house, pointed to a bottle of wine from a local winery and Pabst Blue Ribbon metal collector's tray we had missed, and I took special pains to show her my flower, herb, and vegetable seed collection. I had updated my website where it would clearly show these items for sale. She thanked me for showing her the seeds and giving her some forewarning and said, "If the trackers had seen these, they would have been on the phone in an instant to me." I assured her that we wanted to cooperate, but that this was a way I was hoping to make a little money to help us get by while Dave was in Phase One. "They may want to take samples to take back to the lab," Sherrie warned us.

"That's fine," I replied, "I will give them whatever seeds they need to test." It would turn out that the seeds were an issue that required *another* meeting of all the drug court officials. For some, it still remained unresolved on August 3rd, the day Dave pled guilty to the charges in exchange for being allowed into the drug court program. As he stood before the judge, there was some confusion with some of the other drug court officials regarding my selling seeds.

The judge looked impatient, "We discussed this already."

"Yes your honor, but we didn't actually *vote* on it," one of the drug court officials in attendance said.

The judge pursed her lips in frustration, "Does your wife put out a catalog, Mr. Shuck?"

Dave dodged the question slightly, "She sells the seeds on her website, your Honor, and the seeds are all listed there." He put his head back down and stared at his shoes.

"Fine, fine. She understands she must submit any seeds for testing upon request and we've discussed this enough and agreed. It's done."

The judge then took Dave's guilty plea and directed him to report to the program on Friday, August 7th. It would later be delayed a week due to a scheduling conflict. Dave first official day of drug court was Friday, August 14th, 2009.

We had officially been accepted into one of the most difficult, intensive, and long-term drug diversion programs in the country. If Dave could complete it successfully, the charges against him would be dropped and his records sealed. In 16 months, possibly more, possibly less, Dave would walk away from this with a clean slate and no felony conviction.

Interested in reading more? You can find this book and more by visiting my website: http://christineshuck.com.

About the Author

A self-described auto-didact and general malcontent, Christine lives in an 1899 Victorian in the middle of Historic Northeast Kansas City. Her home has been owned by five owners over the past 100+ years, three of which lived in the home and were also writers, which makes it officially The Writer's House. There's some good writing karma 'round there.

A Missouri native, Christine has also lived in Flagstaff, Arizona as well as in San Francisco and San Jose, California.

Christine writes cross-genre, but within the same shared universe (so far). A complete listing of her books and short stories can be found on her author website.

She and her husband are also renovating two smaller homes adjacent to their property for future rental or Airbnb purposes.

You can also follow her adventures by visiting her blogs:

- Author website and blog: *http://christineshuck.com*
- The Cottages: *http://cottagebb.com*
- Gardening and more: *http://thedeadlynightshade.com*
- Education and Parenting: *http://learningadvocate.org*

All Published Works

Christine writes cross-genre and all of her books can be found on her website at http://christineshuck.com.

<u>Non-Fiction</u>:

Get Organized, Stay Organized – 2008

The War on Drugs: An Old Wives Tale – 2012

<u>Fiction</u>:

War's End: The Storm – 2010

War's End: A Brave New World – 2014

Gliese 581: The Departure – 2016

Schicksal Turnpike - 2018

Don't miss out!

Visit the website below and you can sign up to receive emails whenever Christine D. Shuck publishes a new book. There's no charge and no obligation.

https://books2read.com/r/B-A-BOLF-USRU

BOOKS 2 READ

Connecting independent readers to independent writers.

CPSIA information can be obtained
at www.ICGtesting.com
Printed in the USA
BVHW031146081121
621082BV00005B/85

9 781386 139300